Education, Child Labour and NGOs

Education, Child Labour and NGOs

Prachi Shirur
Srinivas Shirur

SHIPRA

Rs. 995

ISBN: 978-81-7541-347-4

2008 Impression
First Published in India in 2007

Education, Child Labour and NGOs

Published by:
SHIPRA PUBLICATIONS
LG 18-19, Pankaj Central Market,
I.P. Ext., Patparganj, Delhi 110092, India
Ph.: +91 11 22235152/6152, 9650028065
Email: info@shiprapublication.com
Website: www.shiprapublication.com

To
Our Parents
with Love

Preface

Even after 59 years of Independence, India has the largest number of child workers in the world. It also has the distinction of having the largest number of children who never went to school. In spite of many efforts, primary education and child labour are not high on the political or administrative agenda. The state is aware that trade and commerce, the manufacturing sector, merchants and landowners, and the middle class have a vested interest that at least 100 million children should not go to school but should remain in the most dehumanizing and menial jobs. The state is also not serious about implementing the payment of minimum wages to adults and oversees the destruction of all that goes to make up sustainable livelihood for the poor. The consequence of all this is that the poor children have no participation in education and play, and thus loose their childhood in order to complement their family income. Thus, there is a silent conspiracy towards tolerating and perpetuating child labour.

Children are the only hope if we want to change the divided, damaged and conflict-ridden world. If you do not give them the opportunity to participate, they will not acquire the skills. The question is not merely giving them the chance early but also to give them an equal opportunity to succeed in life. That is where; eradication of child labour becomes important.

This book is divided into seven chapters.

Chapter 1 introduces the problem of child labour, its magnitude, causes and consequences, the governmental (Indian Government's), initiatives taken in this regard as also the role of NGOs in dealing with the issue of child labour.

Chapter 2 is an attempt towards developing an understanding of NGOs. Here, NGOs have been defined, its types, functions, relative advantages and constraints compared to the government agencies as well as their role in the development process has been outlined. NGOs have also been distinguished from social movements in this chapter.

This is important since many NGOs have originated from movements. Briefly the role of NGOs in civil society has also been dealt with. With the States gradually withdrawing from social sector and welfare activities, NGOs are being seen as an alternative. However, it has been pointed out in this Chapter that governmental and non-governmental agencies are complementary to each other and one cannot replace the functions of the other.

To understand the NGOs working for combating child labour in Delhi, it is important to locate it in the overall perspective of the NGO movement in India. Chapter 3 attempts just that and traces the history and growth of NGOs in India, their sources of funding and limitations and their relationship with the government.

In Chapter 4 survey report of 17 NGOs has been presented. Here the aims and philosophies, strategies/initiatives, and future plans of these 17 NGOs in a comparative manner have been described. The Chapter also covers the difficulties faced by them in the course of implementing child labour projects.

Chapter 5 and 6 presents case studies of two NGOs viz. Bandhua Mukti Morcha (BMM) and Salaam Baalak Trust (SBT), where the origin and development of these two NGOs, selected for intensive study have been traced. It describes and critically analyses their philosophies, aims, objectives, initiatives, organisational history, structure, sources of funding, relations with the government, police, local authorities, their future plans, successes and limitations.

Chapter 7 concludes the study by analysing the findings of the research and stresses on the fact that NGOs have their limitations and hence to be more effective in the protection and rehabilitation of child labourers, they need a supportive role of the government. It also gives certain recommendations of the tasks, which the government and NGOs should do, in this field. Above all it concludes that the ideology adopted by an organization towards the problem shapes the strategy that it adopts for tackling of the issue.

The fieldwork was carried out in the Capital City of Delhi. Delhi was chosen not only because we reside here but also because we intend to know what efforts are being carried out for child labourers and potential child labourers[1] by the non-governmental organisations in a typical urban centre. Rapid urbanisation and strong and pervasive

* We consider children living in the slums who neither go to school nor work as potential child labourers.

presence of urban poverty is associated with the phenomenon of street children. A crucial segment of exploited child workers who are not covered by any legislation or social welfare programmes are victims not of natural disaster or war, but of urban civilisation – rapid modernisation, unbalanced economic policy leading to rural impoverishment, breaking up of extended families and extreme poverty.

The study is empirical and data has been gathered based on the interviews- formal and informal- with key persons and members of the NGOs and the beneficiaries of these organisations. We have also made use of the brochures, annual reports and other documents produced by these NGOs on the aims and objectives, ideologies and strategies.

The research is confined to studying the various interventions of NGOs dealing with child labour in Delhi. To get an account of the activities of the organisation, the hindrances in their functioning, their opinions regarding some of the best examples of reforms in the field of child labour as also their views on what more needs to be done and finally their future plans, a schedule was prepared and the heads of the organisations concerned were interviewed on that basis. For an in-depth analysis of the two organisations viz., BMM and SBT, we adopted participant observation technique along with the use of interview-schedules. We supplemented primary data with secondary sources of information in the form of documentary material taken from the file of the organisations i.e., brochures, pamphlets, child-sponsorship forms, magazines and Annual Reports.

A documentation of the experiences of the interventions of NGOs in helping child labour is important since many such experiences are scattered and are not studied systematically. It is necessary to carry out such studies and examine the replicability of these models.

In the absence of systematic information on new approaches in various parts of the world, policy makers and practitioners in governmental and non-governmental organisations have had to operate in isolation and learn by doing rather than on the basis of documented knowledge. It is, therefore, desirable to gather information on who is doing and what is being done, both to provide concerned policy-makers and practitioners, with easy access to information, to facilitate communication and interaction among them and to enhance the capability of regional and international organisations, to provide increased support for national and community efforts on behalf of children.

Acknowledgement

It was as much an emotional endeavour as it was intellectually inspiring to write a book on Child Labour. We have tried to cover most of the important NGOs in Delhi who are working in this field. It was indeed a great privilege to interact with great personalities like Swami Agnivesh, Chairperson of Bandhua Mukti Morcha and Ms. Praveen Nair of Salaam Baalak Trust. We are indebted to them for permitting us to conduct an in-depth study of their organisations. We would also like to thank Mr. Melvin (CRY), Mr. Joseph Gathia (Centre of Concern for Child Labour), Ms. Rita Panicker (Butterflies), Mr. T.K. Mathew (Deepalaya), Ms. Jaya Srivastava (Ankur), Mr. Rajeev Haldar (Prayas), Ms. Anju Sharma (Asha Project), Father A. Rajamani (Delhi Brotherhood Society), Mr. S.P. Singh (Bal Sahyog), Mr. Kailash Satyarthi (SACCS), Ms. Mohini Prakash (Mobile Creches), Mrs. Rashmi Mishra (Vidya), Mr. Jugnu Ramaswamy (Street Survivors India) and Mrs. Raka Sinha (Angaja Foundation) for their readiness to share the required information with us.

We are thankful to Prof. M N Panini of JNU, New Delhi in guiding us in this project. We would like to thank our respective organisations, IILM and CSDMS for their cooperation and encouragement in completing this project. The quality of this book has been considerably enhanced by suggestions from our publisher. If we should inadvertently miss out anyone, please accept our advance apologies.

Finally, loving thanks to our parents, relatives and friends for supporting us in this effort.

Prachi Shirur and Srinivas Shirur

Acknowledgement

Contents

1

Child Labour: Nature of the Problem

Less developed countries have always faced the problem of population explosion, thereby increasing the pressure on the natural resources of the country. Huge population has always been considered as a handicap for rapid economic growth because most of the income is utilized in consumption and hardly anything is left for investment. Hence, the simple solution is to restrain the population growth through force with the use of state machinery. This has been implemented successfully in China by their one-child-per-family policy. But this has lead to other problems of increasing number of illegitimate children and abandoned children. In case of India, it was not possible to curtail population by force due to its democratic set up. As a result, population growth of 2.2 per cent could not be solved. This has lead to poverty and thereby leading to child labour. No one can deny that child labour has a close relation with poverty. We are writing this book on the premise that although poverty may be the cause of child labour but removal of poverty is not a pre-condition for abolishing child labour. In fact, reverse may be true. Abolishing child labour can remove poverty by increasing the wages of the adult labour force in the economy thereby increasing the family income. This may encourage adult members to put these children in school because they may be in a better position to bear the burden.

Child labour has been defined in various ways as per the agenda of the institutions-corporate sector, government and NGOs — which are defining it. The meaning of child labour depends on whether its eradication is on moral ground, economic reasons or political expediency.

NGOs like Bandhua Mukti Morcha take a moral ground holding that child labour per se is unjustifiable on both political and economic grounds. That is why they want to define child labour as anyone below the age of 14 who is not regularly attending the school. This is an attempt to interlink poverty, education and child labour.

On the other hand, institutes like International Labour Organisation (ILO) and Government of India (GOI) prohibit child labour in hazardous industries on health grounds. This is the middle ground taken by these institutions to prohibit child labour in hazardous industries for political expediency and allocating them to work in non-hazardous industries for economic reasons.

People in industries, especially those who employ these child labour tend to justify it by arguing that they are merely helping the poor family by hiring their children.

Developed countries take child labour as a human rights issue and justify closing their markets for Less Developed Country's (LDC's) products on moral high grounds that LDC's are able to manufacture these products at low price by exploiting children. They even claim that LDC's governments, by allowing child labour are indirectly subsidising local industries to dump their products in developed countries. Although they have some justification in this argument because by deliberately not willing to implement Minimum Wages Act and Anti Child Labour Act, local governments are indirectly subsidizing the local industries. This argument has been used by developed countries as an excuse to restrain entry of LDC's exports to developed countries on one pretext or other.

Eradication of Child Labour

We are of the view that child labour should be totally banned i.e., it should neither be allowed in hazardous nor in non hazardous industries. The main arguments for this line of thought are as follows

1. Instead of high population becoming a handicap, it is now a great asset. The future development of any country depends on human resources available with that country. Noble laureate – Robert Solow has shown that 80 percentage of economic growth should be attributed to technological growth which is mainly due to skilled manpower. Only 20 percentage of the weightage in economic growth could be

attributed to natural resources and physical capital. Countries like Japan and Sweden are facing huge manpower scarcity due to stagnated or reducing population. This is hindering their economic growth. In contrast, India has a great advantage due to the fact that 75 percentage of its population is below the age of 30. This will prove to be a great potential factor for emerging economies like India. But this potential needs to be harnessed properly. Only if the Manpower is of good quality — physically and intellectually – can that become as asset. Otherwise, it will be a liability. In order to improve the quality of the manpower, government will have to invest heavily in education. Also the government will have to bring child labourers back to school. It is of utmost importance to locate good talent available in various skills from every nook and corner of the country and nurture them properly.

2. Politically also, it is justified to abolish child labour completely. Most of the child labourers are concentrated in rural areas, and mainly belong to Scheduled Castes (SC), Scheduled Tribes (ST) or minorities. Without bringing them to the mainstream of political and economic fields, the dream of participatory democracy may never be realized. One can hear quite often that most of the vacancies reserved for SC & ST remain unfilled because of the lack of qualified people. Ultimately these positions either remain vacant for years or have to be filled by non SC & ST candidates. Till government makes efforts to bring these child labourers to the mainstream, SC & ST candidates will never be able to take benefits of all the schemes launched by the government.
3. One of the main defenses advanced by politicians is that child labour is a necessary evil which can not be practically abolished because in such a case, more number of families will come under poverty line and there will be more hunger deaths. This argument has no justification. Child labour is employed because they are cheap and by employing them, the hirer can make extra profit. There are many families, where parents and elder brothers are unemployed but children are working. This situation could be changed if

'Minimum Wage Act' could be implemented effectively and state could effectively implement 'Employment Guarantee Programme' with least leakages. Once children are out of the labour force, adults will get jobs and also the overall salary will increase. This may give additional incentives to the family to put their children in schools. In the long run, this may prove beneficial to the parents because after education, children will earn better and will be able to support them much more effectively.

4. In the globalised economy, abolishing child labour has additional rationale. According to global consultancy firm – Price Waterhouse Coopers (PWC), India will emerge as the second largest economy along with USA by 2050, with China taking the number one slot. India will witness the highest growth of 5.2 percentage in 2005-50 against 3.9 per cent of China and Brazil while USA and Russia will grow at 2.4 per cent during this period while UK, France, Germany and Japan are projected to grow at less than 2 per cent. PWC is of the view that India's booming working age of 15-59 years will fuel the growth. According to a UN report, while India would witness 0.8 percentage growth in the age group of 15-59 in 2005-50, China would face a decline by around 14 per cent, Japan by 15 per cent and USA by 16 per cent. Hence comparative growth of India hinges on the way it utilizes its manpower in the long run. In the short run, allowing child labour may camouflage poverty to a certain extent because child may complement family income but in the long run, this may adversely affect the quality of manpower which is the key to growth. Allowing child labour may ultimately lead to these children becoming a burden on the nation when they become adult and demand state support in terms of unemployment allowances or productive employment. Many studies have supported the inverse relationship between child labour and poor educational status.

Following chapters will deal with practical problems involved in dealing with child labour. The role of government, international agencies, NGO and society at large will be discussed.

In order to understand the rationale for this study, it is necessary to introduce certain underlying factors and concepts connected to child labour.

1. Child Labour: Definition and Magnitude

Child labour is simply the single most important source of child exploitation and child abuse in the world today. The overwhelming majority of working children are in developing countries in Africa, Asia and Latin America. But pockets of child labour also exist in many industrialised countries. Numerous children work in occupations and industries, which are dangerous and hazardous. They are found in mines, in factories making glass bangles, matches and fireworks, in commercial agriculture, in service sector as vendors, domestic workers, and coolies. The list is endless, as are the hazards and consequences.

However, the distinction between 'child labour' and 'child work' made in the research and policy-oriented literature indicates that not all child work is bad as some work helps in the socialisation of children. 'Child labour', on the other hand involves one or more of the following elements: (i) work by very young children; (ii) long hours of work on a regular full-time basis; (iii) hazardous working conditions (physically or mentally); (iv) no or insufficient access, attendance or progress in school; (v) abusive treatment by the employer; and (vi) work in slave-like arrangements (bonded labour).[1]

1.1 Definition and Categories of Child Labour

Child labour is most comprehensively defined as follows:

A working child is a child in the age range of 5 to 15 who is doing labour, either paid or unpaid, and is kept working at any hour of the day within or outside the family: basically, a child who is deprived of the right to education and childhood.[2]

What makes this definition significant is that it points out that all out-of-school children are child labourers in one form or another. It does not make a distinction between children working in the so-called hazardous industries and children working as part of family labour. If child labour has to be totally eliminated then we must take a holistic approach to children and not categorise them: we cannot condone the fact that some groups of children work and not others. However, to understand the kind of work that children are subjected to in different sectors, the following typology[3] may be of use:

Child Labour: "Those children who are doing paid or unpaid work in factories, workshops, establishments, mines and in the service sector such as domestic labour". Since the law prohibits the employment of children below the age of 14 in factories, mines and other hazardous employment, all such children, except those who work in the service sector or as domestic labour, can be assisted legally.

Street Children: "Children living on and off the streets, such as shoe-shine boys, rag-pickers, newspaper-vendors, beggars, etc." Found working in the informal sector of the economy, the problem of street children is somewhat different from that of child labour in factories and workshops. For one thing, most children have some sort of home to go back to in the evenings or nights, while street children are completely alone and are at the mercy of their employers. They live in the *dhaba* (small eating-place), on the pavement, in the bus terminal or on the railway platform. They are at the mercy of criminals, drug addicts and the police. They have no permanent base and are constantly on the move. So their problem is more acute than that of children working in a factory and living at home.

Bonded Children: "Children who have either been pledged by their parents for paltry sums of money or those working (mainly in rural India) to pay off the inherited debts of their fathers". Bonded children are in many ways the most difficult to assist because they are inaccessible. If the *dhaba* owner has bought them, they cannot escape. If the landlord in the village owns them, they will spend their life in servitude till they get married, and can in turn sell their children.

Working Children: "Children who are working as part of family labour in agriculture and in home-based work". If children are working 12-14 hours a day along with their parents at the cost of their education, their situation is similar to that of children working for other employers. In fact children, particularly girls, are expected to take on work burdens by parents in complete disproportion to their strength and abilities.

Neera Burra[4] adds the following fifth category of children in this typology.

Children Used for Commercial Sexual Exploitation: Many thousands of young girls and boys serve the sexual appetites of men from all social and economic backgrounds. Direct links between the commercial sexual exploitation of children and other forms of exploitative child labour are numerous. Factories, workshops, sweatshops, street corners, railway stations, bus stops and homes where children work, are common sites of sexual exploitation. The physical and psycho-social damage inflicted by commercial sexual exploitation makes it one of the most hazardous forms of child labour.

1.2 Magnitude of Child Labour

While there is no accurate accounting of how many of the world's children contribute to their families or to their own economic support, the number of working children is surely in the hundreds of millions globally. Statistics on child labour are elusive not only because of the special and practical difficulties involved in the design and implementation of child labour surveys but also because of differences in perception about who constitutes a child, or child work or child labour. In India, on the one extreme, is the official definition of child labour, which limits it only to that in which worker gets monetary returns. On the other extreme, are those who include in this definition all those who do any work, even part time or help at home, even if they go to the school. Yet others take into account the socio-economic conditions.

Estimation made by International Labour Organisation (ILO) in 1998, points out that developing countries alone account for 120 million working children (between 5 to 14 years of age). The vast majority of all child labourers live in Asia, Africa and Latin America. More than half of them (61 per cent, according to ILO estimate of 1998), can be found in Asia alone, although their proportion is declining in South-east Asia, as per capita income increases, basic education spreads and family size decreases as also the number of child labourers.

The economic exploitation of children is rampant in India. The 2001 Census put the number of child labourers to 12.66 million whereas the figure is 11.28 million as per 1991 census. As percentage of total workforce, there has been a slight decrease from 5.37 to 5 per cent between 1991 and 2001 census. Unofficial estimates, are however, much higher, ranging between 44 million to 100 million. The Operations Research Group (ORG), Baroda, an organisation involved with market and social research, through an all-India Child Labour Sample Survey commissioned by the Ministry of Labour in 1980-81, had put the figure of working children at 44 million. It defined a working child as "that child who was enumerated during the survey as a child falling within the five to fifteen age bracket and who is at remunerative work, may be paid or unpaid, and busy any hour of the day within or outside the family".[5]

Concern for Working Children a voluntary organisation in Bangalore, estimated about 100 million children as workers.

The National Consultation, organised by the Indian Council for Child Welfare, in collaboration with the UNICEF, suggested that all children who do not go to school should be considered as working children. On this basis the figure would be 90 million.[6]

According to the Bandhua Mukti Morcha Chairperson, Swami Agnivesh, the country has about 65 million child labourers.

Some of these estimates may be highly exaggerated, as they seem to be affected by a deep concern for the child labour. However, the fact remains that there are a large number of child workers in India. At the same time trend of entry of children into the labour force is increasing and the age of entry into the labour force is falling. Sexual exploitation of children is also increasing phenomenally. The working children spend most of their lives employed in unskilled occupations in dangerous conditions, abused and often in bondage. They work for long hours for minimal or no pay.

Even taking the official figures into consideration, one can derive few conclusions. As per 2001 census, the states which have done a good job in reducing incidence of child labour are Andhra Pradesh (–2.28%), Karnataka (–1.90%), Orissa (–1.5), Tamil Nadu (–1.22) and Gujarat (–0.98). Problem is taking a dangerous proportion in most backward states of India. The incidence of child labour has increased in the following states – Sikkim (+ 6.86%), Chattisgarh (+6.96%), Jammu & Kashmir (+6.62%), Jharkhand (+5.47%), Uttaranchal (+3.24%). Broadly speaking, the table – 1.1 clearly shows two major trends. One is that most of the southern states have succeeded in reducing child labour while most of the northern – especially Hindi speaking belt has shown marked increase in the incidence of child labour. Second trend is that states which have better governance, law & order and economic growth had succeeded in reducing child labour.

Table 1.1

State	*Child Workers 1991*	*Child Workers 2001*	*% Workers 1991*	*% Workers 2001*	*Change 1991-2001*
Andhra Pradesh	1661940	1363339	9.98	7.7	-2.28
Arunachal Pradesh	12395	18482	5.65	6.06	0.41
Assam	327598	351416	5.46	5.07	-0.39
Bihar	942245	1117500	3.99	4.68	0.69
Chattisgarh		364572		6.96	6.96
Delhi	27351	41899	1.27	1.35	0.08
Goa	4656	4138	1.95	1.82	-0.13
Gujarat	523585	485530	5.26	4.28	-0.98
Haryana	109691	253491	2.55	4.78	2.23
Himachal Pradesh	56438	107774	4.55	8.14	3.59
Jammu & Kashmir		175630		6.62	6.62
Jharkhand		407200		5.47	5.47
Karnataka	976247	822665	8.81	6.91	-1.90
Kerala	34800	26156	0.58	0.47	-0.11
Madhya Pradesh	1352563	1065259	8.08	6.71	-1.37
Maharashtra	1068418	764075	5.73	3.54	-2.19
Orissa	452394	377594	5.87	4.37	-1.50
Punjab	142868	177268	3.04	3.23	0.19
Rajasthan	774199	1262570	6.46	8.25	1.79
Sikkim	5598	16457	5.18	12.04	6.86
Tamil Nadu	578889	418801	4.83	3.61	1.22
Tripura	16478	21756	2.29	2.79	0.50
Uttar Pradesh	1410086	1927997	3.81	4.04	0.23

NSS survey report number 538 of 1999-2000 shows that incidence of child labour in rural areas is 9.3 per cent whereas it is only 0.4 per cent in urban areas (See table 1.2). From these figures, one can conclude that incidence of child labour is many fold higher in rural areas than in urban areas. As rural areas are intimately related to agriculture, hence it is not possible to eradicate child labour unless government takes steps to modernize agriculture and shift the main source of employment to rural non agriculture avenues.

Table 1.2: Incidence of Child Labour Across Indian States

State	*NSS (1999-2000; Principal and Subsidiary Occupations)*			*Census 1991*
	5 to 9 (rural)	10 to 14 (rural)	10 to 14 (urban)	
Arunachal Pradesh	2.7	25.1	0.7	12.5
Assam	0.4	4.6	0.8	5.7
Bihar	0.2	5.0	0.3	4.3
Gujarat	0.7	11.6	0.4	7.1
Haryana	0.1	2.6	0.2	3.0
Himachal Pradesh	0.6	8.1	0.2	4.8
Karnataka	1.1	15.2	0.6	11.1
Kerala	0	0.7	0	0.6
Madhya Pradesh	0.3	10.6	0.3	9.9
Maharashtra	0.8	8.5	0.2	8.1
Orissa	0.4	9.0	0.2	8.5
Punjab	0.5	5.5	0.4	3.6
Rajasthan	2.5	16.7	0.5	7.8
Tamil Nadu	0.4	8.6	0.5	5.9
Uttar Pradesh	0.2	6.4	0.6	4.8
West Bengal	0.4	8.8	0.6	4.8
India	0.7	9.3	0.4	6.4

Source: National Sample Survey Report No. 458 (Emplyment and Unemplyment Situation in India, 1999-2000), and Population Census as reported in Thorat and Sadana (2001).

2. Sectors of the Economy that Employ Child Labourers

Children are employed in almost every aspect of human work and life. Generally, they are employed in agricultural sector, helping in agricultural operations like sowing, weeding, harvesting and threshing. According to Dube,[7] in rural areas when a boy reaches the age of 10, he is expected to know how to handle a wooden plough, reap the harvest, cut and bring the fuel from forest, and sell and purchase articles in the market. Similarly, a girl of that age is expected to be proficient in weeding paddy fields, harvesting, cooking meals, fetching water, taking care of her youngsters, sweeping and washing the house. A tribal boy begins taking the cattle out for grazing by the time he is 6-7 years old. He also participates in the food gathering activities and learns how to hunt animals and catch fish.

In urban areas, children are engaged in more diversified activities such as loading unloading, hawking, looking after parked vehicles, rag-picking, shoe-shining. Besides, they are also employed as helpers in tea-shops and auto-repair shops or are engaged as domestic servants. They are employed in house and road construction works, brick-kilns, stone breaking, etc.

Few occupations, such as domestic services, street trades, jobs in the hotels, restaurants and various other shops are common for children everywhere.

Child labourers are also engaged in small enterprises of the informal sector, which use indigenous technology and are relatively labour intensive; where workers skill can be acquired outside the schooling system. According to the Labour Bureaus Report[8], children are entrusted with light work in plantations of tea or coffee, such as weeding, manuring, care of nurseries, harvesting, plucking of tea leaves and picking coffee, and so forth. In *bidi* industry, they roll the *bidies* and assist the adult workers. In handloom and carpet weaving, children help the weavers by working in the middle of the loom. In the glass bangle industry, children are employed for doing light duties in the process of manufacturing bangles or assisting the adult workers as helpers. In factories, they are usually employed in packing, pasting, labelling, etc. They also work in mica factories, wood and cork, furniture and fixtures, printing, publishing and allied traders, diamond and other precious stones' cutting and polishing, leather and leather products, rubber and rubber products, machinery, transport equipment and personal services like laundries, dying and cleaning.

They are also employed in some specific industries, which emerge at some specific locales due to socio-economic and geographical conditions. Thousands of children work in the carpet weaving factories of Kashmir, Mirzapur-Bhadohi, lead mines of Madhya Pradesh, printing presses and match box units of Tamil Nadu, handloom centres and garages of Maharashtra, tea and coffee plantations in the south and north-eastern parts of the country.

3. Causes of Child Labour

Child labour is the cumulative effect of a number of factors. Poverty is widely recognised as one of the main causes of child labour, since children are often required to make significant monetary or labour contributions to their families — contributions that may be critical for family survival. Poverty also hinders school attendance because of costs associated with schooling — both direct costs such as costs of books, uniform, etc., as well as opportunity costs such as lost income. Indeed, most of the child labourers belong to poor, landless and semi-landless families, whose income is otherwise, insufficient to keep the family alive. According to a study, 92 million out of 228 million of India's children are in the families below poverty line.[9] This is because of the iniquitous distribution of land. According to the Government of India Report on Child Labour, the lower 50 per cent households own only 4 per cent of the land. In a study of child labour in Kashmir, Ali noted that 97 per cent of children came to carpet weaving in Kashmir due to poverty.[10] Extreme poverty forces people to take loans by pledging their young children who work with the masters for very low or no wages till the loan is paid. The social customs and obligations like births, marriages, death in the families and drinking habits play an important role in compelling the poor to resort to borrowing. Indebtedness becomes an economic inevitability and child labour and exploitation a way of life to many of them. In a study of the Sivakasi match factory, M.N. Kulkarni reported that the "child in 'womb' is pledged to the factory and consumption and maternity loans are obtained on the undertaking that the child born, girl or boy, would work for the factory".[11]

Social forces such as their low-birth seal the fate of many child labourers. The Scheduled Castes, Scheduled Tribes and other backward classes are the main victims of the child labour problem. In a study of Surat textile industry, U.C. Sahoo noted that 86 per cent of child workers belonged to Backward Castes while it was negligible for the upper caste group.[12]

Demographic factors like size of the family also compels children to participate in the labour force. The larger the size of the families that are poor, greater is the tendency of seeking employment for younger people for their own maintenance as well as that of the families.

The problem also persists because employers prefer children to adults for various reasons. Children are more amenable to discipline and control. They can be coaxed, admonished, pulled up and punished for defaults without jeopardising relations.[13] Children are not organised on lines of trade unions which can fight for their rights, not unionised and thus are paid a minimal wage to work for long hours. Children are paid substantially lower wages than their adult counterparts on the pleas that they are less efficient, their requirements are less and they are learning the job. This keeps the cost of production low.

Sometimes, even the poor parents want their children to work, as they perceive several advantages in child's taking up a job. They feel that the job disciplines them, terminates their dependency protects them against the infection of delinquent culture.[14]

Absence of compulsory education is another major factor behind prevalence of the practice of engaging children to work. Many children are forced to stay at home because their parents cannot afford the prescribed minima of uniform, books, stationary and so on. Besides, in the remote areas of the countryside, schooling facilities are scarce and inaccessible.

Unemployment is also a strong deterrent and disincentive to the weaker sections in putting their children to schools. In our country, the agricultural workers are engaged maximum for 290 days in different agricultural and allied works, and are idle for the remaining period, which compels them to engage their children for small sums. Also the increasing volume of unemployment among the educated youth erodes faith in the value of education.

City-ward migration is yet another factor. The progressive mechanisation of agriculture has lead to the squeezing of farmlands out of this sector, thus forcing people to migrate to cities. Migrant children account for around 20 per cent in urban areas.[15] They come to urban areas to avoid economic helplessness and poverty at their villages. Field studies show that the migrant conditions encourage child employment.

Inadequate legislation coupled with insufficient enforcement, is also responsible for the continuation of child labour. The employees succeed in the evasion of the existing laws for the protection of children due to inadequate inspection machinery evolved by the state.

The prevalence of child labour is also blamed on the State's failure to spread the social safety net and the administrative machinery. The absence of social security measures compels some children to work consequent upon the death of their parents/guardians. Children, who leave their homes due to ill treatment of their relatives like drunkard father, step-mother/father, etc., have to join the labour market in the absence of child welfare programmes.

4. Impact of Child Labour on Children

The problem of child labour involves various far-reaching socio-economic consequences. It deprives the children of the opportunity for education, play and recreation, stunts their physical growth and their development for adult responsibilities. Child labour not only disfavours general physical growth, but also leads to defects and ailments. Different types of labour produce different kinds of ill effects. Though some industries are intrinsically hazardous, in many cases, an industry may not be intrinsically hazardous, but it becomes so because of lack of precautions or because no care is taken of the surroundings.

The health hazards in some of the industries are summarised in the Table 1.3.

Table 1.3: Health Hazards

Sl. No.	*Occupation*	*Health Hazards*
1.	Bidi Industry	Chronic Bronchitis & T.B.
2.	Glass Industry	Asthma, T.B., and Eye defects, Bronchitis
3.	Handloom Industry	Asthma, T.B.
4.	Zari & Embroidery	Eye defects
5.	Gem Cutting and Diamond Cutting	Eye defects
6.	Construction	Stunts growth
7.	Rag Picking	Tetanus, Skin diseases
8.	Pottery	Asthma, Bronchitis, T.B.
9.	Stone Quarries	Silicosis

Source: *Children in Darkness* (A Manual on Child Labour in India by Rural Labour Cell of Academy of Gandhian Studies, Hyderabad), 1988, p.13.

The age of a child labourer, many a times, makes a job hazardous which is not so for adults. This includes occupations like domestic work, working in restaurants, where children are at the mercy of employers and consequently in a hazardous situation. The employer often pushes children beyond their physical capacity. This exploitation also includes sexual abuse, which harms the psychological development of these children.

When children labour, besides health, their education also suffers. The future of a working child is endangered as he/she cannot go to school, or is bound to leave school before time, or is unable to coordinate the two activities. In most cases a working child lacks fundamental general and professional knowledge, which is required for normal mental and intellectual development and to prosper in the social and occupational fields.[16]

Child labour has an important economic consequence. The entrance of children into the labour market results in the maintenance of low wages for the labour force as a whole, and increases the adult unemployment and under-employment. Child labour results in a permanently weakened and damaged labour force. Since it involves the use of labour at its point of lowest productivity, it is an inefficient utilisation of labour force.

Certain social implications follow from the economic effects of child labour. The adult unemployment leads to iniquitous distribution of income, which in turn leads to labour displacement, migration, the break-up of family and kinship bonds and competition for survival. In the external work or jobs accomplished in the streets the child is exposed to social perils and even crime, such as drugs and prostitution. Thus, child labour is economically unsound, psychologically disastrous, and physically as well as morally dangerous and harmful.

5. International and National Efforts to Tackle Child Labour

5.1 Efforts Made at International Level

Until recently, child labour was not an issue of major concern, at either the national or the international level. The problem itself was viewed with a mixture of indifference, apathy and even cynicism. It was so widely practised that many accepted it as part of the national order of things. For others, child labour was equated with child work, excused with the argument that work is good for children and a means of helping families. This is no longer the case. Today, child labour is one of the dominant issues of our time. It has now shot up to the top of the global agenda and consumer concerns in both developing and industrialised countries. Corporations are reacting to consumer and other pressure in rich countries demanding corporate responsibility from manufacturers to respect human rights, including the ILO's Conventions on worker's rights and child labour. World-renowned manufacturers such as Levi Strauss, Reebok, Sears and others in the sporting goods industry are now looking into the conditions under which their products are being produced.

At the international level, there has been considerable discussion as to whether global competition rules should require the implementation of certain basic international labour standards, including the progressive elimination of child labour. But there has been wide agreement on the need for intensified action against child labour with an immediate attack on the worst abuses. This change in attitude has led to some remarkable changes in the behaviour of the major actors, particularly governments. Many governments, such as Brazil, India, Indonesia, Kenya, Nepal, Pakistan, Philippines, United Republic of Tanzania, Thailand and Zimbabwe have embarked on a review and updating of national legislation on child labour and adopted practical policies and programmes on child labour. The ILO's International Programme on the Elimination of Child Labour (IPEC) is now operational in more than 25 countries. More than 100 countries have ratified one or more of the International Labour Conventions, which provide protection for child workers in specific occupations or sectors. Today a large number of both industrialised and developed countries have adopted child labour legislation that, on the whole, is progressive and reasonably close to international standards. While many improvements remain to be made, a legal foundation has for the most part already been laid.

The most important developments made towards tackling the issue of child labour in the last few years can be summarised as follows[17]:

1. The media seems to be paying increasing attention to child labour. This enhances the public debate and clearly places the issue on the international policy agenda and on the agendas of individual countries and governments.
2. Greater public attention, as well as, increased efforts by donor agencies and governments to contribute to workable solutions, has encouraged more NGOs to pay attention and dedicate resources to this issue. In addition, many more studies on child labour are being conducted. On a community level, more local schools have been built for working children, more awareness campaigns are being launched on the hazards of child labour and there is more consultation and coordination among local NGOs to combat child labour.
3. International organisations with expertise in children's issues and labour matters have expanded their commitment and the

number of efforts/projects to eliminate the exploitation of child labour. They have forged innovative partnerships between governments, NGOs, the private sector and local communities — all pre-requisites to accomplishing the goal of eliminating child labour.

4. The ILO's International Programme on Elimination of Child Labour (IPEC) is now conducting hundreds of projects throughout the world. In addition to the German government, which provided the initial financing for IPEC, the US and numerous other nations now contribute funds to IPEC's programmes worldwide. UNICEF is developing and implementing educational strategies to get more children into quality primary school. UNICEF and ILO have drafted a letter of intent that will provide a framework for cooperation between the two agencies in the areas of child labour policy development and research as well as technical cooperation at the country level.
5. Interest in child labour has spawned action by consumers of industry worldwide. Consumer groups in many countries actively disseminate information on products made by children under exploitative conditions. Many Multi-national Corporations are developing codes of conduct to prohibit the use of child labour as defined by ILO Convention 138.
6. There is a growing debate by many governments and in various international forums on the problems and solutions to the exploitation of child labour.
7. Additional governments are introducing legislation to make primary education compulsory. Others are raising the number of years children are required to attend school or the minimum age for compulsory education.

5.2 Efforts Made at National Level

India has a long history of legal protection given to the working children. Although, child labour is not banned in toto in India, and nowhere is there an outright ban on the employment of children under a certain age, there does exist an outright prohibition of bonded labour and employment of children in hazardous industries. However, there are areas where no legislation exists such as in the unorganised sector — agriculture, domestic services and the urban informal sectors which place them at high risk of maltreatment, denial of basic human rights and lack of access to those who could help them.

There are both Central and State enactments on child labour – the former covering mainly employment in industries and mining, and the latter covering shops and establishments. India has also signed some of the declarations and agreements prepared by the ILO. The Indian laws and the ILO conventions mainly deal with four matters – (i) minimum age for employment of children; (ii) medical examination of children; (iii) maximum number of hours of work; and (iv) prohibition of night work for children.

The Indian Constitution contains provisions for protection of children from work, which is beyond their capacity, or involves long hours of work interfering with their education, recreation, rest and overall physical and mental development.

Article 15 (3) of the Constitution empowers the state to make special provisions for women and children. Article 23 prohibits traffic in human brings and *begar* and other forms of forced labour. *Article 24* provides categorically that "no child below the age of 14 years shall be employed to work in any factory or mine, or engaged in any other hazardous employment".

Apart from the fundamental rights related to children, certain directive principles in the Constitution direct the State policy and action in relation to child rights, including employment and education children. *Clauses (e) and (f) of the Article 39* states that:

a) The tender age of children should not be abused and citizens should not be forced by economic necessity to enter avocations unsuited to their age and strength;
b) Children should be given opportunities and facilities to develop in a healthy manner and in conditions of freedom and dignity and that childhood and youth would be protected against moral and material abandonment.

This article is substantiated by other articles such as *Article 45* which directs the State to ensure compulsory education for all children under fourteen years and *Article 47* which requires the State to raise the level of nutrition and the standard of living of its people.

Protection is also available under various industrial acts and labour laws enacted from time to time. The provisions relating to the age for admission to employment, regulation of working hours and conditions of employment and appropriate penalties and sanctions for effective enforcement form part of all the relevant labour and industrial laws. Some of these laws are: The Employment of Children (Amendment) Act, 1949; The Plantation Labour Act, 1951; the Employment of Children (Amendment) Act, 1951; The Mines Act, 1952; the Factories Amendment) Act, 1961; The Bidi and Cigar Workers (Condition of Employment) Act, 1966; The Radiation Protection Rules, 1971 made under The Atomic Energy Act, 1962; The Employment of children (Amendment) Act, 1978; The Shops and Establishment Act in various states; and the Child Labour (Prohibition and Regulation) Act, 1986.

The most comprehensive of all the laws is the Child Labour (Prohibition and Regulation) Act of 1986, that prohibits the employment of children (5-14 years of age), in jobs that are hazardous to their lives and health. It also prohibits engaging children in night shifts, making them work in more than one shift, prevents their working near dangerous machinery, handling hazardous chemicals, etc. The working conditions of the employment of children are regulated in all occupations and processes where their employment is not prohibited. The Act also ensures that they have adequate hours of rest and holidays.

A number of other initiatives and programmes have been undertaken during the last two decades, with the basic objective of dealing with the problem of child labourers. The formulation of a National Child Labour Policy, 1987, the enactment of the Child Labour (Prohibition and Regulation) Act 1986, the setting up of a Task Force on child and labour and the ratification of the Convention on the Rights of the Child have all formed a part of this process. The Government is also implementing an ILO programme entitled "*International Programme for the Elimination of Child Labour*". The programme aims at pooling together the resources of the government and those of the non-governmental organisations in an attempt to encourage, promote and support action-oriented programme.

The most significant step in the recent past (December 10, 1996) was the Supreme Court Judgement which fulfilled the legislative intention of the Child Labour (Prohibition and Regulation) Act, 1986. the Judgement aimed at abolishing child labour in occupations specified in the Act as well as implementation of free and compulsory education for all children until they attain the age of fourteen. For every child employed in the contravention of the Act, the court has stipulated that the employer must pay a sum of Rs. 20,000 into a "Child Labour Rehabilitation-cum-Welfare Fund", which would form a corpus whose interest would be used for the child concerned. Besides this, a job in lieu of the child's would be offered to an adult member of the child's family. The government is also obliged to contribute Rs. 5000 to the fund if it is unable to provide alternative employment to an adult in the child's family.

Inspite of the existence of plethora of laws on child labour and the various measures initiated to curb the evil, child labour is prevalent on a large scale in India. The fault lies partly with the loopholes and weak enforcement of laws and partly with the belief systems of the society which lead to an indifference towards child labour problem on the part of the Government, employers and parents.

One of the major criticisms of the legislation on child labour is the lack of uniformity. These laws do not conform to a single agreed minimum age. The minimum age differs from Act to Act, state to state and industry to industry. This is true not only of the definition of minimum age, but also the working hours, rest periods, night employment.

Protective labour legislations do not cover girls. The work in domestic sectors, and other non-industrial sectors where majority of children work, are excluded from labour legislations.

A major loophole in the Child Labour (Prohibition and Regulation) Act, 1986, the most comprehensive Act to date, is that it exempts child labour in family enterprises from the ban. Thus, it permits employment of children in hazardous processes if a process is undertaken by any of their family members. (Here, "family", in relation to an occupier, means the individual, the wife or husband as the case may be of such individual, and their children, brother or sister of such individual)[18]. That is why many clever employers have installed looms for carpet weaving in the homes of the children employed by them. *Bidis*, too, are largely manufactured this way. Also, since people have become aware of this law, they freely claim parenthood of the children they employ.

Weak enforcement machinery in the form of small inspectorate of laws related to child labour is another factor for the failure to implement such laws. The penalties are very light for transgression of laws. The offenders are not worried about deterrent punishment because they can always bribe the Labour Commissioners. When the employers get advance notice of the visit of commissioners, they entrust 'safe' jobs to the children. The law is also evaded thus to non-awareness of the existence of laws, and illiteracy, of the people. Added to all this is the fact that the trade unions are passive towards the interest of the child labourers. Thus, the peculiar socio-economic environment prevailing in the country makes it difficult to eradicate child labour. Hence, there is a need for a total ban on child labour.

6. NGO Intervention in Dealing with Child Labour

The non-progress in the direction of achieving success to solve the problem of child labour, leads one to look towards NGOs for action. NGOs have a vital role in this field since they have flexibility, ingenuity and conviction to identify needs and gaps in public action and to initiate and implement cost-effective programmes for the protection and assistance of the working children. Regarding the need to involve communities in projects related to child labour, NGOs have an especially important role to play. They often have detailed knowledge of local conditions and are closer to community members than government institutions. NGOs can also be more creative, thereby inventing and implementing new approaches to protect children.

Key areas where NGOs can and have already demonstrated effective strategies include removal and rehabilitation of child labourers, public awareness and sensitisation, social mobilisation and environment building. During the last two decades, NGOs have played a strong advocacy role in campaigning against child labour and providing services to working children and their families. Experiences have shown that projects and programmes encounter problems associated with the reality faced by child labourers' families – in particular, poverty affects the success. This is why the need to replace the child's income or labour contribution to the household and to encourage attendance in school of poor children by providing economic incentives, either in cash or in-kind. The economic incentive programmes being implemented by the NGOs[19] may involve the following activities:

- Income-generating activities for families or communities
- Income-generating activities for children ("safe work"), apprenticeships, informal schooling or school-work combinations
- Increasing school attendance by providing food, cash stipends, clothing, books, waiver of school fees
- Income grants to children or families with the specific purpose

to eliminate or reduce child labour

- Non-formal education (NFE), recreation, camps etc. that break the cycle of children
- Other community development programmes (awareness-raising etc.)

6.1 Income-generation for Families and Communities and Other Community Development Programmes

Income-generating activities for families and communities include support for micro-enterprises, credit schemes and employment training for mothers and/or fathers. They are designed to improve the economic situation of families and communities, and thus make child labour less necessary. Regarding cost-effectiveness, income-generating activities are not designed to be welfare schemes but to give families tools to escape poverty. Therefore, when successful, they have a sustainable impact on a whole group of people, not only the targeted child.

6.2 Apprenticeships, Imparting Vocational Training in Schools, School and Work Combination and "Safe-work"

These different approaches for children are all practical, emphasizing skill acquisition and the need for children to obtain practical working experience. However, these are not suitable for very young children, but they may provide a relevant option for older children.

As a mechanism to assist working children, apprenticeships have been widely used, both positively and negatively. They can be merely additional mechanisms to exploit children, in which employers provide training for children, but often without payment. Apprenticeships have also been used as a mechanism for employing underage children. The use of apprenticeships in a controlled situation, however, can provide a very positive mechanism for teaching literacy and job skills.

In the school-work combinations programme, children go to school for example in the morning, and work during the afternoon to earn some money. School can have flexible hours to enable children to work and include, for example, vocational training components in the curriculum to support the work.

Income-generating activities for children which provide "safe work" as a transition to education have received more interest lately because it has become better recognised that child labour cannot be eliminated at one go but is a process that would take its own time. Therefore, an improvement in the working conditions of children is increasingly being seen as one step in the right direction. However, the catch is that this kind of approach promotes child labour.

6.3 Alternative Approaches: NFE, Recreation Activities and Residential Camps

The alternative approaches to combat child labour are designed to break the cycle of child labour and help and ensure entry into school. These activities do not replace any income children forego, but they have the purpose of persuading children to reduce their hours of work or to leave their work altogether. These types of activities are frequently implemented in combination with other activities, such as sponsorship in the form of payments in-kind to increase school attendance, non-formal education, motivation camps and recreation. Sponsorship enables child labourers to attend school, and non-formal education, motivation and recreation activities motivates children to leave jobs, as has happened in the Ranga Reddy District of Andhra Pradesh (India) due to the efforts of M.V. Foundation, discussed later in this chapter. However, follow-up activities which involve taking stalk of the situation to see to it that the children who left their jobs after residential camps, have not taken up the jobs again are a must in such programmes.

In India, the NGOs concerned with the problem of child labour, may be, and in some cases, are involved in the following tasks:

1. Keeping vigil over the enforcement machinery at all levels in order to ensure that the child labour laws are applied in their true spirit.
2. Conducting survey in their areas of operation to identify child labourers and working conditions and to evolve suitable and innovative programmes for health, nutrition, education, recreation, etc. geared towards the overall development and growth of working children.
3. Building pressure through the press and media regarding the employment of children in hazardous occupations.
4. Drawing public attention to the practice of child labour.
5. Participating in government programmes of child workers.

6. Monitoring programmes in their areas of operation to ensure that the benefits actually reach child workers and are not cornered by vested interest.

Few NGOs are implementing some interesting and useful programmes for working children in non-formal education, vocational training, recreational facilities, health and nutrition and have also set up examples for others to follow.

6.4 Education Experiment by M.V. Foundation

Here, it is interesting to note the efforts made by the M.V. Foundation, an NGO in Andhra Pradesh (India). The M.V. Foundation provides replicable model to be followed by the government and other non-governmental agencies. It demonstrates that social mobilisation can achieve the desired results. Parents do not want to exploit their children. Even the poorest want their children to be educated, to better themselves and escape from the poverty stranglehold that they are trapped in. The Foundation also helps in exploding the myth that poverty is the principal cause of child labour and that child labour cannot be totally eliminated till poverty is rooted out.[20]

The M.V. Foundation, in the rural areas of Ranga Reddy District in Andhra Pradesh, is working towards the abolition of child labour through making mainstream education accessible to the children, since 1991. Creating the right climate to achieve their goals, M.V. Foundation began by building up close contacts and relationships with the immediate community: parents and schools teachers, employers and administrative officials, women's groups and local youths. Involving them in each process and drawing on their interest and goodwill, a major breakthrough was made. From one unit — Shankarpally Mandal — M.V. Foundation has now extended its activities to 10 district administrative units covering over 400 villages. Today, 80 per cent of all children in the age range of 5-8 years are in school in these villages. Sixty villages have been made completely child labour free, with every child in the age group of 5-14 in school. And 30,000 working children, including 3000 bonded children and 5000 adolescent girls are receiving education.[21]

The process of social mobilisation began in 1992, drawing on the support of the local people, and with the organisation of education orientation camps, bridge camps and night schools. Most importantly,

M.V. Foundation identified child labourers and established direct contact with each child through local youth volunteers.

The night schools played the role of identifying the hard-core child labourers and creating the right atmosphere for discussing the issue of child labour and education. Simultaneously, there were village-level meetings, public meetings, poster campaigns and cycle rallies by the youth to build an atmosphere where the parents would feel confident about sending their children to school and where landlords were persuaded to reconcile themselves to the fact that children would no longer be available as bonded labourers. This activity was also given an organisational form by forming parent-teacher associations at the village-level and *mandal* education committees at the *mandal*-level.

The mechanism used by the M.V. Foundation has been to enrol the children in the 5-8 years age group into regular government schools with the help of youth volunteers and provide for an additional community teacher to work in government schools along with government teachers. The community sponsors the Foundation's teacher and pays 50 per cent of the salary. The 9-14 age-group children are identified through the night schools and admitted into government-run residential hostels, wherever these exist. Through the bridge courses, MVF is able to prepare children of different age groups through an accelerated learning programme to enter the formal school system. The bridge courses have been important in that these children need to be away from home in an environment which is conducive to study, when staying at home could mean slipping back into doing odd jobs and not concentrating on their studies. Parents' committees have been set up to monitor the running of both the village schools and the hostels.

From the stage of its inception, the strategy of M.V. Foundation has been to put the elimination of child labour on a non-negotiable agenda. It has never used the incentive of income-generation activities for parents, midday meals, supplementary incomes or stipends to wean the children away from work. It has depended entirely on the community's change of attitude towards their children. Building up community-based initiatives and making the community responsible for the programme has established it on a firm footing. The educational bureaucracy — in other words the school authorities — is now accountable to the community. Protest marches, petitions to the education authorities demanding accountability from teachers, have resulted in strengthening community schools.

The success of MVF shows that if properly motivated, children are willing to go to school. It shows that by sustainable strategies and strengthening people's participation, communities can be mobilised to getting children out of work and into school. Most importantly, it demonstrates that child labour can be eliminated without the eradication of poverty. And thus, it is not just the success story of a NGO but also the role model, upon which future strategies may be based. However, it is unfortunate that inspite of its success, its strategy has not been replicated at a wider scale in India, neither by the government nor by the NGOs.

The issue of child labour and solution to the issue, like any other developmental issue, depends on mobilising the competencies of not only the governmental organisation but also private business and non-governmental organisations, in a complementary way. The government, business and voluntary sectors represent three mutually dependent yet in some ways opposing, forces within society. Government is society's instrument for maintaining stability and for reallocating resources from one group to another for public purposes. Business is its instrument for mobilising private entrepreneurship to produce and distribute goods and services in response to market forces. Voluntary action is its instrument for insuring a constant process of self-assessment, experimentation and change in accordance with the evolving values of people. The society that lacks any of the three is a deeply troubled society. The major international assistance agencies have demanded that assisted countries stop using the power of the state to constrain the essential development function of the business sector. In this context, David C. Korten[22] has rightly argued that, it is equally important that they, (international assistance agencies), demand an end to the use of state power to constrain the development and effective functioning of the NGO sector in its unique role as social and political catalyst.

REFERENCES

1. Richard Anker and Helina Melkas, *Economic Incentives for Children and Families to Eliminate or Reduce Child Labour*, International Labour Office, Geneva, 1996.
2. Khatu, K.K. et al, *Working Children in India*, Baroda, Operations Research Group, 1983.
3. Typology extracted from the *State of the World's Children*, UNICEF, 1997.
4. *State of the Worlds Children*, UNICEF, 1997.

5. K.K. Khatu, et al., *Working Children in India*, Operations Research Group, Baroda, 1983.
6. B.S. Padmanabhan, 'Whither Child Rights', *The Hindustan Times*, December 8, 1994.
7. Leela Dube, The Economic Roles of Children in India: Methodological Issues, in Gerry Rodgers and Guy Standing (eds.), *Child Work, Poverty and Underdevelopment*, ILO, Geneva, 1981, pp. 189-94.
8. *Report on the Child Labour in Indian Industries*, Labour Bureau, Ministry of Labour, Government of India, Simla, 1981, p. 7.
9. S.K. Tripathy, *Chid Labour in India*, Discovery Publishing House, New Delhi, 1986, p. 26.
10. I. Sharma, Bipin Kumar, K.B. Padmadeo, 'Child Labour in India: An Anatomy', in B.P.Singh and S. Mukherji, (eds.), *Children at Work: Problems and Policy Options*, B.R. Publishing Corp. Delhi, 1993, p. 23
11. Kulkarni, M.N., 'Match-making Children in Sivakasi', *Economic and Political Weekly*, Vol. XXVIII, No. 43, 22 October 1983.
12. U.C. Sahoo, 'Child Labour in Surat Textile Industry', *Social Change*, September 1990, Vol. 20, No. 3, p. 33.
13. *Report of the Committee on Child Labour*, Ministry of Labour, Government of India, December 1979, p.58.
14. Ibid., p. 10.
15. S.R. Kasbekar, 'Children of Lesser Gods?', *The Economic Times*, 29 July, 1993.
16. IYC/Ideas Forum Supplement 21, *Children and Work*, International Labour Office, Geneva, p. 5.
17. "*By the Sweat and Toil of Children*, Vol. II: The Use of Child Labour in U.S. Agricultural Imports and Forced and Bonded Child Labour", A Report to the Committee on Appropriations, US Department of Labour Bureau of International Labour Affairs, 1995.
18. Child Labour (Prohibition and regulation) Act, 1986', *Indian Labour Journal*, Vol. 28, No. 8, August 1987, p. 1142.
19. Richard Anker and Helina Melkas, Economic Incentives for Children and families to Eliminate or Reduce Child Labour, International Labour Office, Geneva, 1996.
20. *Report of the Committee on Child Labour*, Ministry of Labour, Government of India, December 1979, p. 8.
21. Neera Burra, *Child Labour Impact Assessment Manual*, The Royal Norwegian Embassy, New Delhi, 1997.
22. David C. Korten, *Getting to the 21st Century: Voluntary Action and the Global Action*, Oxford & IBH Publishing Co. Pvt. Ltd., New Delhi, 1990.

2

Towards an Understanding of Non-Governmental Organisations

This chapter conceptualises the role of NGOs as catalyst of social change and explores the potential of NGOs as actors in public policy formulation and implementation in the country. In order to develop insight into the roles of NGOs, an attempt has been made in this chapter to understand and analyse NGOs, their types, functions, advantages and disadvantages in relation to the governmental agencies. The main purpose is to highlight the role that NGOs perform in society especially in the context of the articulation between civil society, state and the market.

NGOs are modern institutions to address to a particular problem and cannot be misinterpreted with traditional institutions like temple trusts, caste *panchayats*, etc. They are new institutions trying to solve old problems. When the social structure is unable to provide certain objectives regarded as necessary, NGOs are established to fulfill the same. They are goal-oriented organisations. However, such organisations do not work in a vacuum, they need the existing social structure for their functioning.

There is dialectic between the state and NGOs. The state finds it necessary to use NGOs when its organisations cannot deliver goods, or when sensitive data have to be collected or to do things that may prove controversial. On the other hand, if the NGOs succeed, that itself is a comment on the ineffectiveness of the state and the masses may get alienated from the state. From some experience, it can also be said that NGOs may come up against vested exploitative interests that have the protection of the state.

A major reappraisal of the role of the state is currently under way throughout the world – in the developed countries of North America, Europe, and Asia; in the developing societies of Asia, Africa, and Latin America; and in the former Soviet bloc. Prompted by dissatisfaction with the cost and effectiveness of exclusive reliance on government to address the social welfare and developmental challenges of our times, efforts have been launched to find alternative ways to respond.[1] With globalisation and privatisation of the economy world over, the state has started withdrawing from some of the core sectors of public services like education, health, employment or other basic infrastructure. The changing social and economic realities coupled with declining confidence in the capabilities of government have recently placed new demands on the civil society institutions especially NGOs.

In the political domain, civil society development is now deemed crucial to stimulating the public pressure and participation necessary to force poorly functioning state institutions to become more responsive and accountable. In the social and economic domains, a more diverse, active civil society is now held out as necessary to cushion the effects of restructuring to ensure public understanding and support for market reforms, to ensure that privatisation does not lapse into cronyism and to connect newly empowered local governments to citizens.

1. Civil Society and the State

Before proceeding further, it is imperative to have an understanding of the concept of civil society and the debate surrounding the state and civil society. The term 'civil society' has been debated around the world as it has aroused both hope and confusion.

The hopes generated by civil society is an outcome of a common knowledge that it can promote, further and sustain 'public good'. On the other hand, confusion abounds because there is a lack of consensus on what constitutes a civil society, the typology and its relationship with numerous other societal actors.

The recent popularity of the term – civil society – can be seen in conjunction with a marked shift in the perceived and actual roles of the state. Not only has the state and its various arms undergone major shift in terms of roles and functional outlook, the market has also been undergoing major shift in terms of focus leading to realignments and new ethical underpinnings. While the state and the market occupy two different spheres in society, the third space is increasingly being viewed as 'civil society'.

The idea of civil society is both western and modern. Andre Beteille stresses the importance of citizenship in the conception of civil society. According to him both are complementary and civil society cannot amount to very much where citizenship is absent or weakly developed.[2] Civil society is distinctively a modern phenomenon because citizenship itself is a modern idea and value. There is a great importance of the individual as an autonomous moral and legal agent in the development of civil society. It is the legal recognition and protection of the natural rights of individuals that transforms a political society into a civil society.[3]

The French Revolution marked a watershed in the emergence of citizenship as a socially acknowledged category. But it did not transform the subject into a citizen overnight. Nor was it simply a question of the replacement of the monarchy by a republic. In Britain, where the state underwent a more gradual transformation, citizenship evolved over a longer period of time with changes not only in the laws but also in customs, sentiments and attitudes. The point to be stressed here is that the emergence of citizenship and, with it, of civil society, depends on changes not only in the distribution of power but also in ideas, beliefs and values.[4]

Beteille points out that not every kind of state, but only the modern constitutional state is relevant to the development of civil society. However, the relationship between state and civil society is ambivalent. The state can play a constructive role in the evolution of civil society, as it has done in Britain and the Netherlands; it can also play a destructive role, as it did in Germany and the Soviet Union.[5]

If one closely looks at the dominant conptualisation surrounding civil society, it becomes discernible that the term is used for associations and institutions that have a formal character e.g., voluntary development organisations.[6] It also denotes a non-political space between the household and the state. Here, it is also very important to stress that civil society is a political concept in as much as it is concerned with exercising power to advance and defend the economic, social and political interests of citizens.

Civil society requires for its sustenance a body of rational impersonal rules, and that only the state can be the ultimate guarantor of those rules. State and civil society have to be viewed together, and that very little will be gained if one begins with a negative attitude towards the state. In the words of Beteille, "nothing can be more destructive of civil society ... than the idea that the best way to create and invigorate civil society is to empower the people at the expense of the state".[7] State performs certain indispensable functions, and if those are subverted or undermined, civil society will wither in the bud. The above discussion leads us to conclude that the state and civil society are complementary; they are not alternatives of each other.

2. NGOs: Concept, Types and Functions

The civil society has functioned as a new secular ideology, becoming the building block for a good society which values people, regardless of age, gender, race, disability or other aspects of social background. Advocates of civil society go on to the extent of saying that civil society, if harnessed and nurtured, would transform democracy and reshape the balance of power in favour of greater social inclusion, justice, dignity, equality of opportunity and respect.[8] According to Beteille, civil society would complement the market, creating 'social capital' — the glue that binds people together in relationships — and adding a meaning to people's lives over and above their role as economic producers or consumers.[9]

The question that arises here, is how would this civil society be delivered, and the answer lies in Lester Salamon's 'associational revolution'[10] — the striking upsurge in organised voluntary activity in almost every part of the globe, with NGOs delivering human services, promoting grassroots development, preventing environmental degradation and protecting civil rights. While talking of the associational revolution, it is worthwhile to mention that the presence of such associations is mark of an egalitarian and dynamic democratic society. The American life is so strikingly characterised by voluntary associations that De Tocqueville had remarked: "In no country in the world has the principle of association been more successfully used, or applied to a greater multitude of objects, than in America".[11] .

A whole range of such organisations variously called as Voluntary

Agencies, Action Groups, Grass Root Organisations, Non-governmental Organisations, are now flourishing at a global level. The significance and political clout of these agencies have grown to such an extent that a large number of them enjoy a 'consultative status', with the United Nations (UN) and its specialised agencies. The UN Department of Public Information that directly deals with these agencies term them NGOs and define them as follows. "Non-governmental Organisations are any of those organisations which are not part of government and which have not been established as a result of an agreement between governments. NGOs can be research institutions, professional associations, trade unions, chambers of commerce, youth organisations, religious institutions, senior citizens' associations, tourist bodies, private foundations, political parties, Zionist organisations, funding or development-international and indigenous agencies, and any other organisation of a non-governmental nature".

The UN definition served the purpose of broadening the scope and space for 'voluntary action' at a global level. The voluntary action covers a wide range of activities such as charity, welfare, relief and rehabilitation, provision of services, socio-economic development of poor, human resource development, and so on. Inequality among individuals is a perennial source of motivation for voluntary action in every society. Social services are initiated to help eradicate the inequality and to uplift the underprivileged. The term volunteer is normally used to denote some one who offers unpaid service to a good cause. Philanthropy appears to be an essential motivating factor in the voluntary action. When a sense of social responsibility is being inculcated in the individuals, they take up various steps to improve the condition of the people all around.

Voluntary action, if it is to be socially effective, must acquire some kind of an organisational form. Here, it is pertinent to examine the processes through which voluntary associations become established as the institutional expressions of social movements. According to T.K. Oommen[12], social movements imply the projection of a desirable set of values; it is a project addressed to the future. The rise and fall of social movements indicate that human beings cannot be permanently imprisoned in the present social structure and no eternal moratorium can be imposed on creativity. Wendell King, for example, has identified three phases in the "life cycle" of social movements: the incipient phase, in which a handful of believers work towards a goal established by the founder (often a charismatic leader); the organisational phase, in which voluntary associations are established; and the stable phase, in which the voluntary associations (if they survive) become increasingly professionalised, bureaucratic and conservative.[13]

The development of at least a semi-permanent organisational structure is often essential to the realisation of the goals of a movement. However, such an organisation often sets in motion influences, which defeat the very ideals that gave birth to it. Contemporary sociologists have often pointed out how the idealism and missionary zeal of spontaneous emotional commitment to a cause tends to be "corrupted" by the tendency of all organisations to become "ends in themselves". Max Weber's doctrine[14] of the routinization of charisma, is the leading theoretical statement of this view.

Thus, the basic problem that all social movements face is the inevitable tension between mobilisation and institutionalisation. Movements crystallize when men share beliefs and activities. But what distinguishes them from other similar kinds of social behaviour is institutionalisation — the process of development of a network of relatively stable interaction, normative structure, gradation of participants. Without institution no movement can attain its stability; yet the logical corollary of institution may be the very demise of movement — they may become mere organisations or associations. Therefore, movements may be viewed as institutionalised collective actions, guided by an ideology and supported by an organisational structure. Without mobilisation, no movement can sustain itself, but if these mobilisations are uninformed by an ideology and an organisational basis, they cannot be distinguished from elementary forms of collective behaviour, like panic response. This intermediary stage between clearly formalised structures and vaguely articulated directionless process is that which distinguishes movements from organisations on the one hand and elementary forms of collective behaviour on the other.

There are four essential elements in any voluntary association: (a) method of formation which is voluntary on the part of a group of people, (b) method of government, with self-governing organisation to decide on its constitution, its servicing, its policy and its clients, (c) method of financing, with at least some of its revenues drawn from voluntary sources and (d) motives of profit excluded.[15] Organisations having all the four elements are rare and perhaps are the ideal forms.

Defined in broad terms, voluntary associations include all non-state organisations-churches, business firms, labour unions, foundations, private schools and universities, cooperatives and political parties. Although all non-state, common-purpose organisations with voluntary memberships are voluntary associations, that is, organisations whose existence is dependent upon freedom of association, David L. Sills in the Encyclopaedia of Social Sciences, focussed upon organisations that meet both of two additional criteria. First, the major activity of the organisation is not related to the business of making a living, that is, to the economic activities of its members (as in the case of professional associations, trade unions, or cooperatives). Second, the volunteer (i.e., non-salaried) members constitute a majority of the participants (as they do not in corporations, universities, or foundation, in which the directors or trustees are in a minority vis-à-vis the employees, faculty or students).

However, in this book the term NGOs is defined as a non-political, non-profit, non-religious community organisation governed by its own rules and regulations without external control and initiated for community development. Therefore, all non-governmental and voluntary organisations like those involved in cultural, sports and religious activities or professional and political organisations (like hospitals, university, trade-unions, recreational and sports clubs, religious outfits like *Rashtriya Swayam Sevak Sangh*, churches) need not necessarily be included in the category of NGOs.

As mentioned earlier, the term NGO is very broad and can be applied to any organisation, which is operationally distinct from government. In the field of development, NGOs range from large, northern-based charities such as OXFAM to local self-help organisations in the South.[16] Some large NGOs are an arm of the government, for instance, the Department of International Development (DFID) of the British Government, or Canadian International Development Association (CIDA) of the Canadian Government. Some, on the other hand are extensions of the government, for instance Indian Government has set up development societies using the government fund, as also there are committees to harness watershed management which are part government. NGOs may include research institutes — like Overseas Development Institute (ODI) and Coordinating for Development Action (ICDA) as well as lobby groups such as the World Development Movement.

The last decade of the 20th century may be described as the decade of the NGO since there has been such a massive growth of NGOs in this decade.[17] The upsurge of NGOs is a worldwide phenomenon, although it has become particularly conspicuous in the less developed countries of Asia, Africa and Latin America. In some of these countries, the NGO is seen as the main driving force in economic development and social change. NGOs are now active in practically every field: literacy, education, health, sanitation, child-care, nutrition, habitation, environment and so on.

The NGOs are coming to be represented as the Third Sector of society in which the state and the market are viewed respectively as the first and the second sectors. However, this is a very large claim since, there are a great many things in the life of a society that are not covered by the state or the market, and it is doubtful that NGOs, no matter how numerous or versatile, can do all the things that are not done by the state or the market.[18]

The NGO is distinct from the state because it is a 'non-governmental organisation'; it is distinct from the market because it is a 'non-profit organisation'. But there are many institutions in contemporary societies, such as universities, hospitals, religious organisations, etc that cannot be justly described as creatures of either the state or the market. To the extent that it is inferred that the functions of such institutions can be better performed by NGOs that inference is false and needs to be repudiated.[19]

It is true that because the government has failed to protect a citizen's right to basic needs that the NGOs have stepped in. But there are times when a non-government organisation itself becomes unaccountable, and then it becomes necessary to ask what justification it has to claim to be an interlocutor for the disadvantaged. Given the intricacies involved in actually getting access to funding, a number of NGOs have been set up by ex-government officials or their families. Most of these are NGO only in name; their real purpose is to exploit the jet-setting lifestyle and perks that come with the territory.

There are instances of NGOs functioning under the guidelines of foreign funders at the risk of offending local sensibilities. In a recent instance, an NGO booklet on AIDS used language that was so sexually explicit that the matter went to court. This gave politicians a chance to grab an opportunity to cast themselves in the role of preservers of local culture and heap calumny on all NGOs working in the area.

This is not to say all NGOs are spurious. There are many NGOs in India that work in conditions of extreme adversity to bring succour to the underprivileged. No one can forget the example of Sanjoy Ghose who paid with his life for attempting to better conditions for the poor in Assam.[20]

However, an excess of zeal for their actual or possible contributions to the extreme of a wholesale denigration of the work done by the agencies of the government and by autonomous and semi-autonomous institutions or of the withdrawal of public support and sympathy from them is against the well-being of society.

To have a decent society there must be a balance between the state, the market and the civil society. What we need, in the words of Anthony Giddens, is "a society which has the centrality of the market as a means of producing the most effective economy, but which also has an aggressive, supply-side policy, with government playing a central role in investment in education and in the necessary infrastructure of communications, transport and so forth, making the society able to respond effectively in a more globalised economy. At the same time, a more active, reflective citizenry is very important because it means one can draw upon these wellsprings of activity to produce new relationships between the third sector and the renewed, reconstructed government and the economy".[21]

3. Advantages of NGOs in Relation to Government Agencies

We have already noted that NGOs have the potential of being more effective agents of development than government agencies, at least among the poorer and weaker sections. We now see in what respects NGOs are superior to government organisations.

As against the governmental action, voluntary actions are considered to be more effective in the implementation of developmental programmes as they use a participatory method to raise awareness, mobilise local personnel and resources and they are well aware of the local needs and demands. They are closer to the people and therefore, better understand them. Proximity to the people ensures the latter's involvement in projects. It is also possible for NGOs to monitor the implementation of projects closely and if necessary make corrections in midstream.

Compared to the government agencies, the NGOs are informal, humane, less bureaucratic, rapid and to a certain extent cost effective. They have also the added advantages of flexibility in their structure and operation on the one hand and availability of trained, experienced and dedicated workers on the other. Participation of voluntary organisations in the developmental and welfare endeavours has also the effect of reducing administrative costs as well as checking the wastage of the limited governmental resources.

Because of its relative smallness of scale, the voluntary body is able to experiment, by doing old things in new ways or trying out quite new services, and in doing so takes the risks which might be more difficult for a large and essentially more bureaucratic state concern. This independence in trying out new strategies, as well as the opportunity to concentrate more single-mindedly on particular issues or needs, puts the organisation into a strong position to be a watch-dog in the field in which it specialises. This also gives it a chance to develop and promote creative suggestions for statutory policy.

NGOs also have certain strengths peculiar to themselves. They are by definition, at least in their early days, motivated by personal enthusiasms. They count amongst their supporters, those who are concerned to help individuals with specific disabilities, or who have a particular cause at heart, such as certain legislative or administrative change and find it more congenial or consider it likely to be more effective, to work within a specialist group.

For all these reasons, voluntary bodies have an important potential for the future. However, this potential is not always realised because of several constraints.

4. Constraints of NGOs

K.K. Kuriakose[22] has listed some of the limitations on a fuller NGO participation in development, which are as follows:

1. *Multiplicity of numbers and absence of mutual cooperation*:

Even the smallest of countries boast of the presence of hundreds of NGOs ranging from village based self-help groups to national level organisations. In larger countries like India, Indonesia and the Philippines, the number of NGOs runs into thousands. Not only are the numbers large, they also represent a wide spectrum of interests and subjects. One can rationalise this diversity and spread by saying that the phenomenon represents the richness and diversity of human aspirations at any given moment in the life of a society. However, it makes it very difficult to operationalise a policy of cooperation with NGOs. This constraint is in-built into the situation. When several NGOs are competing for the limited resources, cooperation is bound to take a back seat. Moreover, charismatic individuals who, therefore, tend to develop a certain "vested" interest in preserving the identity of their creations start many small NGOs. They tend to view suggestions for cooperation with suspicion. Development activities today have become more complex, requiring a multi-sectoral and sometimes a macro approach. This is not possible without NGOs cooperating with each other and since they are not so open to cooperation, their ability to play a major role as agents of development also remains restricted.

2. *Scarcity of resources*: The existence of large numbers of NGOs, each trying to obtain as much support as possible, from a limited support base, adds to the problem. Most of the NGOs working at the grassroots level lack the technical expertise, professional competence, organisational infrastructure and capabilities, which restrict their endeavour thereby leaving the influential NGOs appropriate the funds.
3. *Political problems*: A third constraint is the political aspect of development. The emphasis on participatory development has brought into sharp focus the limitations of many NGOs even though they are amongst the most vocal in stressing the importance of participation. Extreme poverty and highly exploitative structures in the developing countries make it impossible for people to exercise their options. Empowerment of people is a precondition to participation. Empowerment of people implies helping people to organise themselves to

develop action programmes that will give them confidence in their capacity to be change agents. Unfortunately, such a course of action is fraught with many risks because of the opposition it is likely to raise. The slightest hint of resistance tends to invite retaliatory action by the rich and the powerful against those who challenge them. Consequently, unless the NGO leaders are ready to pay the heavy price that may become inevitable, very little progress is possible.

4. *Government reluctance*: Yet another constraint is the reluctance of governments to accept NGOs as partners in development. Most discussions on development emphasise the need for the participation of people in the entire development process. It will be difficult to find a government in the developing world, which raises any serious reservations about the role of NGOs to mobilise people to participate in the development process. However, if one took a closer look at the amount of money these very governments make available to NGOs, the findings will be quite disheartening. This unenthusiastic attitude towards NGOs is not only because of many shortcomings of the NGOs but also because of governments' unwillingness to strengthen NGOs especially those which are likely to help people in their quest for empowerment.

   For instance, in India, governments for over a decade now, have been professing the importance of civil society but have done precious little to empower them. A key area, for example, is the funding of the sector. At the moment, the sector remains heavily funded by foreign organisations and is supervised under the Foreign Contributions Regulations Act (FCRA), which was promulgated during the Emergency period (1976) to monitor and ensure that foreign funds are not used for anti-national activities. NGOs for long have been lobbying against the Act and have termed it as undemocratic and violative of human rights. They say that since the threat perception has changed now, to restrict the free-flow of foreign funds to the sector on the grounds that it could be used for anti-national activity is absurd. Despite these protests, the persistence of the Act shows that it is there to keep NGOs in control[23] .

5. *Lack of professionalism*: As a rule except for a limited number of large NGOs, the smaller NGOs lack professionalism in their programming. Quite often professionalism is confused with careerism or full time paid work. That a person can be a volunteer, full time or part time, and yet do a professional job is often not understood by many NGO leaders themselves. Sometimes this lack of professionalism is due to the fact that an NGO is the creation of a charismatic leader who is afraid of losing control of the organisation. This lack of professionalism results in the inability of most NGOs to plan and implement programmes in an efficient manner.
6. *Inability to transform micro-projects to macro-projects*: It is generally recognised that NGOs are successful in carrying out small projects. Often these projects deal with one special area of concern such as poultry training, dressmaking, mother and childcare, drinking water supply, etc. However, when the same NGO has to undertake a much larger project, it seems to falter and fail. Moreover, the needs of development of a local community today cannot be compartmentalised. It is necessary to have an integrated approach, which too most NGOs are unable to establish.

There are certain constraints to the working of NGOs which are as follows:

1. Very often voluntary organisations work in a very small scale or in a small area and their resources are too meagre to meet the widespread social needs of the people for whom they work.
2. There are some obstacles, which often come in the way of proper delivery of services to the people by the people. Although, they might have the best intentions, they often lack the basic preparation, familiarity with the environment, technical knowledge and experience in delivery of services. In many instances, they lack an overall strategy and methodology in evolving and implementing programmes or activities in which they are involved. Also, at times they fail to adapt their strategy/strategies to changing circumstances

in the areas where they work. They enjoy their autonomy or independence and often refuse to cooperate with other non-governmental organisations or with local officials. The local follow-up of their actions is generally improper and insufficient due to lack of personnel or financial resources.

3. Further, most of the voluntary organisations are unstable as they are set up with much enthusiasm and commitment but they fail for one reason or another. In such circumstances, they may not easily be relied upon for their continuous work over a number of years.
4. There is also no surety of continuity to work and employment of the staff in the NGOs; therefore, it cannot really attract the qualified workers. More often a qualified person seeks employment in the voluntary organisation only if he has economic security from other sources or is devoted to the organizational aims and objectives.
5. These organisations are thus ill equipped in terms of sufficient number of qualified staff. Hence, they are unable to maintain the minimum standard of work. This is more evident in the lack of adequate and sustained financial resources. Consequently, they can neither plan their programmes properly nor can they prepare budget estimates to plan their expenditures.
6. The stability of NGOs is questionable also because in most cases they depend on external sources of funding for their existence. The problem of dependency remains because the sources of funds are time-bound. Support is usually given on a project-to-project or year-to-year basis and could easily be withdrawn. In such cases, the ultimate stability of the voluntary sector seems to depend on dedication. Those groups, which persevere, survive from year to year as long as they have the spirit. But in many cases the spirit breaks.

6. NGO-Government Relationship

Apart from the problem of dependency, NGOs also face the problem that of the antagonistic relationship with the government. The conflict exists at the working levels of government in virtually all countries.

In countries where the political and top administrative echelons are supportive of the NGO sector (India and Sri Lanka as is evident from the flourishing business of NGOs here), large segments of the field administration resent NGOs. Several reasons are given for it.

Government officials state that NGOs come into a village and establish their programmes, often without discussing and usually without any attempt to integrate with the government's activities. On the other hand many NGOs believe that governments wish to control them and that the NGOs will lose their autonomy if they integrate more closely. A number of NGOs expressly identify government staff and related officials (from the rural areas, major cooperatives or extension authorities) as one means through which the rural elite gains a disproportionate share of the project funds. Some NGOs are also concerned that close integration with government may appear to give a commitment to political party, or provide NGO support to a development agenda which they would wish to change.

The cause behind the lack of understanding and willingness to cooperate arises from both sides. In a few countries, the conflict is more severe than solely a lack of cooperation. Here, a policy of cooperation may be the official government position, but it is a policy, which is not observed at political or senior administrative levels. Difficult NGO registration, slow approval of NGO projects, insistence that NGO funding be 'additional' to an aid agency's regular programme, a refusal to accept finance for bilateral or multilateral projects that includes an NGO component, legislation with power to prevent NGO amalgamation or to deregister NGOs, are evidence of a de facto government policy of non-cooperation.

There are several possible reasons behind governmental rejection of NGOs. Many NGOs actively criticise government. The resentment created in the lower levels of the bureaucracy is also reflected in the attitude of senior officials. More importantly, however, is that some NGOs are seen to present an alternative political voice in the country. Many governments are unwilling to grant a high degree of freedom to such organisations. Also of concern to politicians and senior administrators is that NGOs are capturing an increasing share of aid funding, thereby diluting the control that governments have over development programmes.

Despite, the above mentioned constraints, NGOs have become an important force in today's world. In this era of globalisation, NGOs operate both at global and at local levels. The global NGOs are transnational, influencing policies of countries. Further, the NGOs are networking with each other; thereby they have created a space for themselves in the global power structure and are emerging as the third force shaping events in the world. This is evident from the protests by the NGOs at the recent World Trade Organisation (WTO) meet at Seattle (December 1999). What NGO demonstrators did outside the Seattle meeting of the WTO was perhaps more important than what ministers did inside. The demonstrators prevented the inaugural session of the meeting from being held, smashed local shops and obliged the authorities to declare a curfew. In the old days, governments would have denounced them as thugs. But this time the United States and several other delegations lauded their idealism, and said the demonstrators had a point in wanting WTO to be more open and more concerned about labour and environmental standards in trade.

This confirms that a great new force has emerged on the world scene. No longer are economic issues debated and decided mainly by governments and corporations. Global networks of NGOs have emerged as a new force that is multinational in corporations and globalised in vision.

Thus, NGOs matter more and more in world affairs. But they are often far from being "non-governmental", as they claim. And they are not always a force for good. This comes out clearly as we go through the following paragraphs.

As already stated, the tag "Non-governmental Organisation", was used first at the founding of the UN. It implies that NGOs keep their distance from officialdom; they do things that governments will not, or cannot, do. In fact, NGOs have a great deal to do with governments and not all of it is healthy.

Here we may mention the example of aid agencies. A growing share of development spending, emergency relief and aid transfers passes through them. According to Carol Lancaster, a former deputy director of USAID, America's development body, NGOs have become "the most important constituency for the activities of development aid agencies". Much of the food delivered by the World Food Programme, a UN body, in Albania during 1999 was actually handed out by NGOs working in the refugee camps. Between 1990 and 1994, the proportion of the European Union's (EU) relief aid channelled through NGOs rose from 47 per cent to 67 per cent.[24]

Governments are also happy to provide that money. Of OXFAM's 162 million pounds income in 1998, a quarter, i.e. 24 million pounds was given by the British government and the EU. Medecins Sans Frontiers (MSF), the winner of Nobel peace prize in 1999, gets 46 per cent of its income from government sources.[25] In Africa, where international help has the greatest influence, western governments have long been shifting their aid towards NGOs. Europe's donors also say that bilateral aid should go to NGOs, which are generally more open and efficient than governments. The UN, too, sees NGOs as indispensable. Most such agencies now have hundreds of NGO partners.

So, the principal reason for the recent boom in NGOs worldwide is that the western governments finance them. Many NGOs are becoming contractors for governments. Governments prefer to pass aid through NGOs because it is cheaper, more efficient and more at arm's length — than direct official aid.

Western governments also use NGOs (mostly multilateral NGOs) for bringing back useful information. Outfits such as the International Crisis Group and Global Witness publish detailed and opinionated reports from places beset by war or other disasters. The work of Global Witness in Angola is actually paid for by the British Foreign Office. In some benighted parts of the world, sometimes only NGOs can nowadays reveal what is going on. The Amnesty International, which is one of the biggest campaigning NGOs on human rights has around one million members in over 162 countries and its campaigns against political repression, in particular against unfair imprisonment, are known around the world.

The most potent sign of the closeness between NGOs and the governments, aside from their financial links, is the exchange of personnel. In developing countries, where the civil service is poor, some governments ask NGOs to help with the paperwork requested by the World Bank and other international institutions. OXFAM has former staff members not only in the British government, but also in Finance Ministry of Uganda. This symbiotic relationship of some of the Multilateral NGOs with western government shows that the former are hardly independent.

One may argue that it does not matter even if NGOs are losing their independence and are, becoming just another arm of government, since many do achieve great things: they may represent the last hope for civilians caught in civil wars, for those imprisoned unfairly and for millions of desperate refugees. But NGOs do have their shortcomings as mentioned earlier. They may themselves become vested interest, may use funds to fatten themselves. Since, aid agencies are far away, they use NGOs to translate their objectives into practice, but some NGOs misappropriate the funds and devise their own methodology of writing false reports. Thus, NGOs can become self-perpetuating. When the problem for which they were founded is solved, they seek new campaigns and new funds. The old anti-apartheid movement in South Africa, when its job completed, did not disband, but instead became another lobby group for southern Africa.

The above discussion does not lead us to conclude that NGOs should resist opportunities to work with governments and official aid agencies. But NGOs should approach these invitations as potential negotiating opportunities to forward their vision of development.

The critical question here is whether the overall project in hand is in the interests of the poor. The NGO might well see that it can do a good job making a project component more efficient, perhaps more socially responsive, but it must guard against strengthening a system which works against the poor.

To conclude, we may say together with John Clark say that voluntary organisations will only achieve their full potential if they develop a more strategic, coordinated way of working. Their projects are important and will remain so, but in themselves do no more than create islands of relative prosperity within an increasingly hostile sea.[26] These projects should not be seen as ends in themselves, but as starting points. They are demonstrations, catalysts, and vantage points. Using them as their base of experience and knowledge, voluntary organisations should help to challenge governments, official aid agencies, international companies and others to change their ways. They should do what they can to promote the evolution of people's organisations and grass roots democracy. And they should lobby developed nations to make the changes necessary for international justice.

REFERENCES

1. Lester M. Salamon, "The Rise of the Non-profit Sector", *Foreign Affairs*, Vol. 74, No. 3 (Summer 1994), p. 111.
2. Andre Beteille, "Citizenship, State and Civil Society", *Economic and Political Review,* September 4, 1999, p. 2588.
3. Gurpreet Mahajan, "Civil Society and Its Avatars", *Economic and Political Review*, May 15, 1999, p. 1189.
4. Andre Beteille, "Citizenship, State and Civil Society", *Economic and Political Review,* September 4, 1999, p. 2589.
5. Ibid.
6. "Seminar on Civil Society and Governance: A Report", August 3, 2000, *PRIA*, New Delhi.
7. Andre Beteille, "Citizenship, State and Civil Society", *Economic and Political Review,* September 4, 1999, p. 2588.
8. Barry Knight, "Towards a Perfect Civil Society", *Alliance*, Vol. 4, No. 2, 1999, p. 28.
9. Andre Beteille, "Citizenship, State and Civil Society", *Economic and Political Review,* September 4, 1999, p. 2588.
10. Lester Salamon, 'The Global Associational Revolution', *Foreign Affairs*, July/August, 1994.
11. Alexis de Tocqueville, *Democracy in America*, Longman, Green, Longman & Roberts, London, 1862, Vol. I. p. 216.
12. T.K.Oommen, *Protest and Change: Studies in Social Movements*, Sage Publications, New Delhi, 1990.
13. Wendell C. King, *Social Movements in the United States*, Random House, New York, 1956.
14. Max Weber, *The Theory of Social and Economic Organisation* (Ed.), Talcott Parsons, Glencoe III, Free Press, 1957, first Published as Part I of Wirtschaft and Gesellschaft, 1922.
15. D.L. Shills, "Voluntary Associations: Sociological Aspects" in International Encyclopaedia of the Social Sciences", Vol. 16, 336-367, Collier-MacMillan, 1968.
16. Overseas Development Institute,"NGOs in Development", Briefing Paper, August 1988, p. 1.
17. Andre Beteille, "The Third Sector: Driving Force in Economic Development", *The Times of India*, 10 March 2000.
18. Ibid.
19. Andre Beteille, "The Third Sector: Driving Force in Economic Development", *The Times of India*, 10 March 2000.
20. Sanjoy Ghose, General Secretary of Association of Voluntary Agencies for Rural development- North East (AVARD-NE) and his dedicated band had addressed themselves to the problem of soil erosion, in the Majuli island of Assam, directly. They had built teams of volunteers to place sandbags along

the banks. Only by such concerted community effort could there be some hope of arresting the devastating floods. All sections of the community got involved, from teachers and the elite to youth who would otherwise be looking to migrate to the nearest town, or at least find a regular job there. This followed other long-term actions – more sustainable ways of building houses, growing different crops, storing food and other belongings differently.

It was this alternative vision that angered the cadre of ULFA. They had established a base in Majuli because of its inaccessibility. They would have drawn supporters from the same alienated youth who were now being attracted to a different path altogether, one that was constructive and not violent by showing people how they could rely on themselves, Sanjoy altered the status quo and this is what probably led to his abduction and subsequent killing.

21. Anthony Giddens, "The Role of the Third Sector in the Third Way", *Focus*, CAF, September 1999.
22. K.K. Kuriakose, In Quest of Development: Role of Non-Governmental Organisations, Vishwa Yuvak Kendra, New Delhi, 1989.
23. Dr. Anil Aggarwal, "Empower Civil Society", *Voluntary Action Pulse*, VANI, January 2000.
24. "Sins of the Secular Missionaries", *The Economist,* 29 January 2000, p. 25.
25. "Sins of the Secular Missionaries", *The Economist,* 29 January 29 2000, p. 25.
26. John Clark, *Democratizing Development: The Role of Voluntary Organizations*, Earthscan Publications Ltd. London, 1991.

3

Non-Governmental Organisations in India

In this chapter we would briefly trace the history and growth of NGOs in India, their funding sources and problems associated with funding and lastly NGOs' relationship with the government. The overview of NGOs functioning at the national level has important implications for the area specific study of NGOs working for child labourers in Delhi.

From an operational point of view, the term NGOs in India has been used to denote those organisations which are non-governmental, voluntary and non-profit making bodies, with a legal status such as a society registered under the Societies Registration Act, 1860 (XXI) or under corresponding State Act or Trusts registered under the Indian Trust Act or Charitable and Religious Act, 1920 or Co-operative Act or Section 5.25 of the Companies Act, 1956.[1] But, the real problem is that under the 1860 Societies Registration Act. Almost anybody can register an organisation and engage in a wide range of activities. Estimates suggest that there are more than 30 lakh registered NGOs in India,[2] but there is no way one can say how many of these are NGOs and how many are not.

The presence of NGOs in India is clearly visible today, than ever before, in the developmental endeavours. The international recognition to the valuable contribution of voluntary efforts in India and the resulting international funding to them, have given a boost to the process of voluntarism and a mushrooming growth of NGOs in India. An estimated 15,000, most of them with a rural focus, are actively collaborating with external donors.[3] The struggle of the fisherfolk against the aqua farms on the east coast and their fight against mega-industries on the west coast, the movement of the tribals for self-rule (i.e., the demand for autonomy), the *dalit* demands for self-respect, dignity and justice, the struggles of women to recover their dignity and rights to productive resources, the campaign and struggle against displacement and destruction as in the case of the Narmada Dam, the forging of many national and international alliances and networks to address these issues at the national and global levels, are representative of this upsurge of democratic activity in India. Thus, the role of NGOs has gone far beyond the boundaries of traditional 'welfare' (i.e., charity and relief) role. The changing role of the contemporary voluntary efforts in the national endeavour could not be analysed in all its dimensions, without a brief recapitulation of the history of voluntary movements in the country.

1. History of Voluntary Movement in India

In India, the history of the development organisations is linked to the history of voluntary efforts and thereby, to the history of social welfare and social reform in the beginning of the 19th century. The religious and social reform movements like "Brahma Samaj", "Arya Samaj" and "Rama Krishna Mission", etc., adopted 'reformist' approaches to eradicate the prevalent social evils and the religious dogmas. Caste rigidity, untouchability, human bondage and inhuman treatment to women and children were some of the evils, which were deep-rooted in the social fabrics of the era. Many literary and educational societies were set up to expose the emerging middle class to secular western thoughts and ideas. Here, the case of the Ramakrishna Mission may be pointed out. It was founded in 1897 by Swami Vivekananda, the chief disciple of Ramakrishna Paramhansa, whose preachings in the 19th century West Bengal provided a rallying point for Social Reform Movement in India. The Mission was founded with the purpose of preparing young persons to dedicate themselves to the service of God by serving humanity. Building of skills of different trades, appropriate values and ethics and insertion into social service programmes in rural and urban areas were the strategies used for the preparation of young people by the Ramakrishna Mission.

The emergence of Mahatma Gandhi during the struggle for independence changed the complexion of voluntarism and began a process of networking of organisations under his leadership. The most decisive action, which gave an impetus as well as a new direction to the voluntary action, was Gandhiji's call for social action to end untouchability, casteism and illiteracy. He called for people's participation at the grassroots level. Gandhiji felt that 'constructive work' was distinct from political work. According to him, sooner or later all development work will turn out to be political work. This is evident from emergence of such organisations like, 'All-India Spinners Association (1925)' and 'All India Village Industries Association (1934)'. Another case in point is the Sewapuri case. Sewapuri[4], represents the history of unique institution inspired by Gandhian philosophy of constructive social work. The first organisation set up here was *Gandhi Ashram* on November 15, 1947. Inspired by the call of Mahatma Gandhi to work in rural areas, several activists of the freedom struggle settled in Sewapuri to initiate the work of *Gandhi Ashram*. In the initial years, the *Gandhi Ashram* focused on *Khadi* and village industries, health and nature cure, agriculture and livestock. In 1951, *Gandhi Smarak Nidhi* was also founded in Sewapuri to promote other activities focused on eradication of leprosy, provision of sanitary facilities and promotion of basic education. Over the years, the work of Sewapuri has resulted in evolution of several principles of voluntary action inspired by the philosophy of Mahatma Gandhi. Non-violence and local self-reliance are the basic themes.

In the initial phase after independence, the legacy of the Gandhian era influenced voluntary action to fulfill the unfinished tasks undertaken before independence (as is evident from the Sewapuri case). The effort to further spread the *khadi* and village industries became not only an important area for voluntary initiatives but also of governmental responsibility. Social action based voluntary work continued in the field of welfare, relief and rehabilitation. In addition, voluntary organisations also participated in the governmental endeavour in the field of agricultural extension, health and rural development.

The next phase could be seen between the mid-sixties to early seventies. This was the period when the development model (trickle-down approach) followed by the government was criticised. The contradictions between the rich and the poor, and the divide between the urban and rural India had increased during the past twenty years of independence. It was at this stage that alternative and integrated rural development began to be experimented, through the initiatives taken by a new generation of people in 1968-69. The response to droughts and floods provided the motivation. For instance, following the serious drought and shortage of water in many parts of the country in early and mid 60s, a unique institution called "Action for Food Production" (AFPRO) was set up in mid-60s primarily with a view to provide drilling for water facilities. Over the years AFPRO has evolved into a technical support institution in areas of agriculture, land management, drinking water, irrigation, biogas, livestock, and so on.

Part of the motivation of this period also came from the changed political circumstances with the defeat of the Congress in several state assemblies in 1967 and the gaining momentum of the students' movement in the 1967-69 period. This was also the period when the 'Naxalite' movement[5] surfaced and gained momentum and reached its peak in the 1969-70 period.

The next phase is the period from the clamping of National 'Emergency' in 1975, though its roots began in the 1974 J.P. movement[6]. This was the period when the circumstances had forced a number of people to reflect upon their experiences or look back critically at the emerging trends in the country's political process. The rise and fall of the Janata Party's government between 1977 and 1979 was quite a disillusioning experience for many. This fall out from the political process contributed to the growth in voluntary action, both in terms of quality and quantity. This was the period when more focused work with target groups, landless labourers, tribals, small farmers, women, scheduled castes, scheduled tribes, also became the basis for the programme of work of NGOs.

Integrated development models soon replaced the fragmented, compartmentalised development, which was still charity and service oriented, in the late eighties. However, structural obstacles at each level of activity and the need to influence related policies gave rise to empowerment models by the early nineties. More emphasis was laid on the structural alleviation of poverty and exploitation, through sustainable development processes by integrating gender, environment and human rights concerns into the process. Together with this, many NGOs began adopting a participatory approach to strengthen self-management and grassroots democracy.

Several NGOs, in particular over the last 30 years, have played a role whereby people and ideas spread to other NGOs and became a basis for new initiatives. They may be called mother institutions. People who spend time in such institutions move out to create new voluntary organisations and thus, these mother institutions become a learning ground, and experimentation took place for another set of voluntary organisations. A few instances that may be cited here are as follows.

Sewa Mandir: Set up in 1969 by Dr. Mohan Sinha Mehta, a well known educationist of Udaipur, in Rajasthan, the aim of the organisation was to promote rural development and adult education among poor tribals of southern Rajasthan. Over a period of time, a large number of individuals worked in Sewa Mandir and moved out to set up their own institutions, some within the district of Udaipur and some within the state, and some beyond, some doing the work at grassroots levels similar to what Sewa Mandir started, some working at grassroots level but with different perspective.

Social Work and Research Centre (SWRC): It was set up more than 30 years ago in Tilonia, Rajasthan. SWRC was based on Mahatma Gandhi's concept that knowledge, skills and wisdom found in villages should be used for their own development before getting skills from outside. Several youngsters from all over the country came to SWRC, Tilonia to get a feel of rural development and many were encouraged to go back to their own regions and states and set up similar institutions. By early 80s, many SWRC's were functioning in states like Himachal, Haryana, Orissa, Tamil Nadu, Rajasthan, etc. They all carried the name of SWRC initially and after a period of time changed their name and identity. But SWRC, Tilonia was the base from where they learnt some ideas about rural development.[7]

Self Employed Women's Association (SEWA): SEWA started as part of a larger trade union – Textile Labour Association – in Ahmedabad, Gujarat, representing the textile workers in that city. Its initial work was organising women workers and initiating struggle for improving their situation. After an initial period of work in organising and struggling for the cause of the women workers, SEWA began to recognise the importance of initiating some developmental efforts, like cooperatives for credit, production and marketing activities in several areas of women's empowerment. The initial work of SEWA in the 70s became so visible and innovative that many other organisations in different parts of the country wanted to imbibe its philosophy and perspective in their own work. They sought affiliation with SEWA, and also got registered as SEWAs in different parts of the country like Delhi, Uttar Pradesh, Bihar and Madhya Pradesh.

These and many such organisations have, therefore, contributed in significant ways in propagating certain ideas and approaches to working with issues of development as well as the very concept of voluntary organisations. These could be seen as pillars around which a whole generation of people working in voluntary organisations has evolved in India.

2. Sources of Funding

Historically, voluntary organisations have acquired funding mainly from non-institutional sources, like funding in the form of donation from the community, richer sections of the society or from philanthropists, etc. In the post-independence era, the non-institutional funding has been limited. The NGOs are greatly dependent on institutional funding sources, i.e., from both the private institutions (like socio-cultural and religious institutions) and government funding. The two most dominant sources of funding to NGOs in India today have been international sources/foreign contribution and the government funding.

2.1 International Funding

Foreign contributions in India are defined as 'the donation, delivery or transfer made by any foreign source of any article, currency or foreign security'. The flow of foreign money to the NGO sector is regulated in India by a legislation, called the Foreign Contribution and Regulation Act, (FCRA), that was passed in 1976. For receiving any kind of assistance from the international donors, the NGOs are required to register under the FCRA, under the Ministry of Home Affairs, Government of India (GOI).

The foreign source of funding is divided into the following categories:

1. *Bilateral Institutional Funding*: It includes aid from agencies, department and ministries of the developed countries such as

USA, UK, Japan, Sweden, Denmark, Norway, Canada and Australia etc. For instance, Canadian International Development Agency (CIDA), Danish International Development Agency (DANIDA), Department of International Funding for Development (DFID), Norwegian Agency for International Development (NORAD), Swiss Development Cooperation (SDC), United States Agency for International Development (USAID), and the like. Bilateral funding is made available to NGOs under the approval of the GOI for the specific programmes and largely regulated by the GOI.

2. *Multilateral Institutional Funding*: This comprises of funds from various agencies of United Nations institutions like World Health Organisation (WHO), United Nations Educational, Scientific and Cultural Organisation (UNESCO), United Nations International Children's Emergency Fund (UNICEF), Food and Agriculture Organisation (FAO), United Nations Fund for Population Activities (UNFPA), United Nations Development Programme (UNDP), International Labour Organisation (ILO), United Nations Environment Programme (UNEP), etc. The other multilateral institutions like the World Bank, International Monetary Fund, also provide funding to the NGOs in India, under the overall supervision and regulation of the Government. It is mainly project/scheme based. This type of funding is very limited and is confined largely to the major NGOs in India.
3. Another category of international funding support is from the solidarity groups, international trade unions, etc of the developed nations. This type of funding is mainly confined to the issues relating to human rights, women and child development and environment and the like. The Bhopal Gas disaster is an example where several solidarity groups in the developed countries raised resources to support local action in India.
4. *International NGOs*: Private NGOs of the developed nations primarily the European and American institutions, foundations, like the Ford Foundation, the Rockefeller

Foundation, provide support to the NGO sector in India. Some examples are: Action-Aid, Cooperative for Assistance and Relief Everywhere (CARE), CARITAS, Christian Children's Fund (CCF), Helpage, Indo-German Social Service Society (IGSSS), Oxford Committee for Famine Relief (OXFAM), and the like. By and large, the major source of international funding to the voluntary efforts in India by the NGOs, is the international non-governmental sector.

The thrust areas of the major international funding have been in the sectors like women and children, health and family welfare, education, environment, rural development, science and technology. Though international funding brings new initiatives, new ideas and approaches in a wide range of areas, however, the international funding has certain limitations. Firstly, it is temporary in nature and for a short duration action oriented projects. As a result, the NGOs work in an atmosphere of uncertainty about the continuation of their projects.

An important issue relating to foreign funding is that of the influence they have on the agenda of voluntary organisations in the host countries. In different points of time, different issues (such as issues of education, health, women and environment), have taken primacy in the eyes of NGOs, partly because they were accorded priority by the funders. In specific sense, many a times the representatives of foreign funding agencies tend to influence openly and directly the programmes and activities of the NGOs, many a times inconsistent with the realities on the ground. The emphasis on projects related to AIDS is a good example. The paranoia over AIDS in the West has led to a concern about AIDS in India, which has a large number of HIV cases. Though, the concern is necessary, but the focus is largely on sexual practices and condom distribution. However it may be pointed out that in India a large number of people face the danger of AIDS through blood transfusions and contaminated injection syringes. But this hardly gets any attention, since the Western nations already have safe practices in operation where things like blood transfusion, or even simple things like administering injections are concerned. However, we do not have such safe practices, and an AIDS programme, conceived in the West, does not reflect our reality.

NGOs, being less bureaucratic and more efficient compared to government agencies, are largely being used by the international donor agencies to fund directly. For instance, with the gradual withdrawal of the government from the social service – health, education, nutrition, water supply, etc – and subsequent privatisation of these sectors, the NGOs are being looked upon as 'efficient implementers' of many components of the Structural Adjustment Programmes. The World Bank is encouraging NGOs to run these projects, in India. This involves a risk of NGOs becoming sub-contractors at the expense of developing local capacity to deal with the problem. But the scenario is not so bleak. Many NGOs have raised their voice against the Bank and many of the changes in the policies of the World Bank, e.g., disclosure policy, environment policy, rehabilitation policy, have been the result of intense campaigning and lobbying by the NGOs and activists, in which many Indian activists and groups (for instance, Narmada Bachao Andolan) took part.

With so much money being pumped up, the NGO sector has increasingly come to resemble the private sector. Increasing fund flows make it easy for some to consider the development option without the pressure of a frugal lifestyle. People come here driven by money prospects rather than by commitment to a cause.

Money does not only define the joining of this field, increasingly it is also tending to define the project itself. So, instead of first spending a lot of time working in a community, and through that figuring out what their needs are and then designing solutions which are appropriate to that particular community, this process is now turned upside-down. In this upside-down version of development work, people who have a certain interest in the field go for whatever project funds happen to be available for.

There are sceptics who perceive a hidden agenda in the 'big business of giving'. Claiming that India has belied the global expectations of a thriving, expanding market, they think the war the developed world is waging on poverty is aimed at bolstering the purchasing power of the people and increasing the number of consumers exponentially. And all is being done to have more buyers for foreign brands.

Criticisms aside, the foreign sources of funding has led to availability of funds for innovation and experimentation, since much of the government funding is tied to schemes and programmes. Below are discussed the different types of government funding and the problems associated with them.

2.2 Government Funding

In pursuance of its policy to support and encourage voluntary efforts, the government at the central level has initiated the programmes providing financial assistance to NGOs through grants-in-aid. The basic purpose of the grants-in-aid is to encourage and promote NGOs in India and particularly in the areas where government action is rather limited. The grants-in-aid are given to NGO sector by various departments and ministries such as Ministry of Human Resource Development; Ministry of Rural Development; Department of Education; Department of Women and Child Development; Department of Youth Affairs and Sports; Ministry of Welfare; Environment and Forests; and Science and Technology and so forth.

A certain limited funding is available with the state governments and at the local institutional level. At the local level, funds are provided largely through the District Rural Development Agencies (DRDAs), Zilla Parishads, Panchayati Raj Institutions, etc.

Besides, many governmental agencies such as National Children's Fund, Central Social Welfare Board, Council for the Advancement of People's Action and Rural Technology (CAPART) provide funding to NGOs. However, they are for specific purposes and are available in a limited scale.

The government funding however, has many intrinsic limitations. They are available for specific schemes designed primarily in accordance with the policies and priorities of the government. It is rarely that a proposal evolved by an organisation on its own receives funding from the government.

At the same time, government funding is limited since the amount of funds available may not provide the overhead, administrative and running cost of an organisation. It can only partially cover the overall financial requirement of the organisation.

Bureaucratisation and control over mechanisms of funding have considerably undermined the autonomous functioning of NGOs.

One of the major constraints of government funding is the procedural delay in timely release of funds. Besides, grants-in-aid sometimes impose conditions for a matching contribution from NGOs working at the grassroots level, which very few can afford to make as a result of this, only reputed and large scale NGOs that can afford such matching grants, have monopolised a major chunk of government funds.

The small NGOs working at the grassroots level, with much of social commitments, dedication, often face a serious financial crisis in their endeavour. Some of them may not be aware of the different funding schemes of the government, while others may lack knowledge of basic objectives, procedures and requisite documents, rules and regulations involved therein. The latter may result either in submission of an incomplete application by them or a poor design of project proposal, thereby, contributing to a procedural delay in release of funds by the government.

The NGOs studied in Delhi also face some of the above-mentioned constraints. These are discussed in chapter 4.

Thus, the issue of funding of NGO sector has become increasingly critical. On the one hand, there is concern related to dependence on external sources of funding — government as well as foreign funding. (Several attempts are being generated to secure alternative ways of financing, as devised by the organisation called Street Survivors of India, discussed in chapter 4). On the other hand, the question of autonomy of NGOs and the issue of funding has been raised. The NGO sector in India currently faces the challenge of ensuring their autonomy, on the one hand and securing a viable and sustainable funding base, on the other.

3. Government vis-à-vis NGOs

As is evident from the above discussion, there is a considerable presence of the state in the existence of NGOs. First, voluntary organisations are subject to laws of incorporation be it as a registered society or a trust or a cooperative society. Second, voluntary bodies being non-profit in character, have to seek formal exemption from income tax which subjects them to regular checks by tax authorities. Third, those NGOs, which undertake to implement government-sponsored welfare and development programmes have to satisfy the authorities about their constitution, managerial capability, accounts, annual reports, etc. Besides, their non-political, non-communal, nonsectarian character has to be certified. Also, they have to enter into a written agreement as prescribed by the government and have to abide by such conditions as the authorities may have laid down. These conditions usually include submission of audited accounts and progress reports. Some NGOs even invite or accept some official representatives to be on their programme or management committees for maintaining effective contact, coordination, and cordiality and often to ensure day-to-day support.

Then there are some voluntary organisations, which raise funds for their work not only from Government but also from outside the country. They have to follow additional prescribed procedures, namely either obtain prior government approval for receiving a foreign grant or if already registered by the Home Ministry under the FCRA 1976, they have to abide by rules governing the receipt and utilisation of foreign money.

Part of the reason behind the government's desire to have greater control over NGOs stems from the 'activist' nature of some of the groups. One major argument on the relationship between the government and NGOs was that there was no opposition to NGO activities as long as its programmes were restricted to various welfare programmes. But the moment any of their activities start jeopardising the local mafia on the contractor-criminal-politician nexus (as it happened in the case of Sanjoy Ghosh discussed earlier), NGOs start receiving threats. This was found true in the present study of the NGOs. Those NGOs, which are into service provision role i.e., engaged in providing the reformist role of provision of non-formal education, recreation and health care, have a smooth sailing with the government and local authorities. But, those engaged in the release and rescue of child labour e.g. Bandhua Mukti Morcha, come in constant opposition with the local authorities and police, as will be discussed in chapter 5.

Thus, as stated earlier, the government has not taken a hostile attitude towards all NGOs. With NGOs that do not challenge the existing power relations, the government has taken a cooperative stance. This becomes clear from the following account of the involvement of NGOs in national development by the government.

After independence, the government of India identified certain areas for state intervention such as health and education, and assumed limited responsibilities in sectors like social welfare. The government provided support to NGOs to undertake projects for the benefit of women, children, and youth, handicapped and destitute through the Ministry of Social Welfare at the central and state level and through government sponsored autonomous bodies.

In the First Five Year Plan, NGOs were identified as social service organisations, particularly in the field of care, protection and rehabilitation of the disadvantaged. The National Institute for Public Cooperation and Child Development (NIPCCD) was established to institutionalise government efforts to promote NGOs in the country. NIPCCD concentrated in the area of training voluntary workers, supporting NGO activities and promoting liaison between government and NGOs. Currently, NIPCCD is the apex body to train functionaries, and to coordinate, monitor and evaluate the Integrated Child Development Services Scheme of the government.

The Third Five Year Plan characterised the NGO action as an aspect of public cooperation. The National Advisory Committee for Public Cooperation (NACPC) came into existence in 1952 with the twin objective of assessing the existing programmes in connection with national development and advising the Planning Commission in this area on an on-going basis. Soon, it was found that NACPC had representatives mostly from national NGOs and many of the member NGOs did not even have grassroots activity. As the public cooperation got institutionalised, NACPC gradually lost its credibility in the eyes of small and comparatively new NGOs.[8]

In 1953, the Central Social Welfare Board (CSWB) was set up under the Union Ministry of Social Welfare with the objective of providing financial assistance, coordination, training, technical guidance, consultancy and promoting NGOs engaged in activities for women and children. In order to reach out to the local NGOs and to respond spontaneously by way of processing applications for grants speedily and releasing funds in time, the CSWB established state level Social Welfare Advisory Boards. An evaluation of CSWB has recorded that it has been reduced to a fund-disbursing agency of the government. This is mainly because of not attending to the main CSWB i.e., objective of providing technical guidance in the form of training, supervision, and consultancy to promote and coordinate voluntary action.

From the middle of the Sixth Plan, there have been a number of initiatives at the government level to insitutionalise a dialogue between the government and NGOs. In this connection, the then Prime Minister had written to all the Chief Ministers in October 1982 with a suggestion to establish consultative group of voluntary agencies to widen the role of NGOs in the implementation schemes under the twenty point programmes. It was envisaged that the periodic meeting of such group would give useful feedback on actual implementation of the programmes and help in sorting out difficulties affecting the work of NGOs. Although, it was a constructive initiative, very few states formed consultative groups. Whenever the groups were formed, the regular meetings were not held because of the absence of proper perspective in the bureaucracy to accept NGOs as an alternative to government strategy to reach out to the rural poor besides the government policy to help the NGOs was not made clear to the concerned government officials. Thus, the move on creating consultative committees of NGOs at the state level met with a natural death.

Another significant move in the field of government-NGO relationship has been the revival of the People's Action for Development India (PADI), which was created as a forum where representatives of national level NGOs with grassroots level rural development work could give feedback to the government. The mandate for PADI was to promote voluntary efforts, channel foreign and national government funds for implementing rural development programmes, and above all protect the interests of the NGOs in the country. In 1983, the Council for the Advancement of Rural Technology (CART) was set up to improve the conditions in rural areas through innovation and diffusion of appropriate technology with the help of NGOs. In 1986, the Council for the Advancement of People's Action and Rural Technology (CAPART) was created, merging CART and PADI, which retained the basic objectives of CART and PADI. CAPART was promoted as an autonomous organisation under the Union Ministry of Rural Development. It is considered to be one of the largest funding bodies in the country. Besides, providing financial assistance to NGOs for executing government designed rural development programmes, CAPART gives grants to NGOs to design projects and to work in rural areas in the field of voluntary action, rural development and rural technology.

In 1986, on the initiative of the Consultant (Voluntary Agencies) to Planning Commission and CAPART, a draft proposal to establish a

Council for Rural Voluntary Agencies and Code of Conduct through an act of Parliament was put forward for discussion. This move was linked with the Seventh Plan document on NGOs and the government's intention to involve NGOs in implementing anti-poverty programmes in rural areas. It was envisaged in the Bill that the NGOs would themselves regulate affairs and establish for themselves a code of conduct, which will become the basis for their own accountability. As a result, NGOs seeking government funds do not have to go through the rigid procedures of getting their proposals cleared by various ministries. This created a lot of debate in the NGO sector. The city based large NGOs were in the forefront of gathering support to reject the move. The group favouring such a move has been arguing that it will bring an end to the dependence on foreign funds, will give equal weightage to the small, medium and large NGOs, and will create a platform to sort out differences between NGOs and the government. The other group argued that a statutory base for the Council and the Code of Conduct was against the spirit of voluntarism, affecting the independence of NGOs and their capacity to project the critique of government policies and programmes affecting the marginalised sections. It was feared that it would lead to more bureaucratisation of NGOs. The issue met with a natural death, on the face of strong opposition from this section of the NGO sector.

Thus, over the different Five Year Plans, the government perspective towards the NGO sector changed from government planning for the NGOs and funding schemes, to government encouraging the NGOs to plan for themselves and advancing financial assistance to them, which is a very positive trend. Former President K.R. Narayanan, in his address to Parliament, said that the new government's development strategy will rest on a 'triad': the government will provide a strong policy and regulatory leadership; the private sector will bring dynamism and efficiency to the economy in a competitive environment; and local democratic institutions and the civil society will be encouraged to bring about enthusiastic participation of the people in the development process. However, it was not indicated how this is intended to carry forward.

Thus we cannot be very hopeful of the future of the NGO sector, since for over a decade now, governments have been professing the importance of civil society but precious little has been done to empower them.

The government has not made any headway towards evolving a coherent policy to this sector. Of the prevalent laws devised for the voluntary sector, there are three Acts that serve to curtail the activities of the sector, namely, FCRA, Societies Registration Act and the Income Tax Act. As mentioned earlier, FCRA was promulgated during the Emergency period to monitor and ensure that foreign funds are not used for anti-national activities. But in reality the Act has been used to keep the NGOs under control. Now that the threat perception has changed it is not appropriate to restrict the free-flow of foreign funds to the sector on the grounds that it could be used for anti-national activity. It is all the more so if one compares the actual amount of funds coming to NGO sector — barely 1 per cent[9] with the funds that are going to the corporate sector. With the liberalisation of the economy, the functioning of the corporate sector has been made easier, since FERA (Foreign Exchange Regulation Act) has been scrapped and the companies in the corporate sector not having to apply for licensing anymore. However, the cumbersome registration process under the FCRA is still mandatory for the NGO sector. It is true that some NGOs have misappropriated the foreign funds, yet the fact remains that misappropriation of funds cannot be controlled by any rigid Act. The important issue is not to monitor foreign funds but to monitor anti-national activity, whether it is undertaken with foreign money or national currency.

The Societies Registration Act is outmoded, and as for the Income Tax Act, the only NGOs it mentions are charitable trusts, thereby completely ignoring the voluntary development organisations which are engaged in development issues, and which too should be exempt from paying Income Tax. The definition of Income for NGOs is not at par with that in the private sector, still in the NGO sector, all receipts are treated as incomes. The government feels that fiscal incentives to promote civil society will be used by business people and others to siphon off their ill-gotten gains. Although, this has been true in some cases, yet the answer does not lie in strangling this sector.

A government truly interested in the civil society would provide tax incentives for Indians willing to fund local institutions as all governments in the western countries have done. This will help and encourage India's civil society to move away from foreign funds. Institutions, like Green Peace International, raise millions of dollars from the public every year for their work. In 1994, individuals in the US donated $105.1 billion (Rs. 4,20,000 crore) to the country's NGOs.[10] India's middle class is also growing rapidly and can be encouraged to give funds for literacy, anti-poverty, community mobilisation, social welfare and environmental efforts. The government must create this financial framework.

If the government really wants to encourage the civil society, it must develop a very healthy respect for the NGOs – in fact, for democracy and plurality itself – and learn to dialogue with it. It is extremely essential to create an environment where the government and the NGOs accept each other as equal actors in the development process, which will prepare them to listen, learn and act on a mutually agreed path.

REFERENCES

1. Manoranjan Mohanty and Biranchi N. Nanda, "NGOs and Funding- Central and Centrally Sponsored Schemes", YUV-Vandhu Cultural Group, Orissa, 1993.
2. Nilanjan Mukhopadhyaya, "Partnership in Crisis", *The Hindustan Times*, October 5, 1997.
3. M.K. Bhat, *Shitfting Priorities: NGOs, Donors and Changing Policies*, in Bhargavi Nagaraja and M. K. Bhat, Building Civil Society, India Civil Society Collective, Bangalore, 2000, p. 65.
4. Sewapuri is the name of a place at Varanasi in Uttar Pradesh.
5. The origins of the Naxalite movement can be traced to the struggle in Naxalbari in the late 60s. The Naxalite ideology was extreme leftism and they believed that revolution is possible only in the rural areas where there is maximum exploitation. They protested against greater concentration of land and regarded the Indian state as an imperialist state.
6. The J.P. movement under the aegis of its leader Jaya Prakash Narayan, a leading socialist of modern India played a significant role in cementing anti-Indira Gandhi forces in 1974 which eventually forged a united front in the shape of the Janata party. The movement (with its call for 'Total Revolution'), which started with protesting against corruption, ended with the demand of the right to recall (i.e., elected leaders have to be accountable to the people) from the falling Bihar government. Finally, the movement itself became corrupt.

7. In october 2000, the Barefoot College, Tilonia, of Rajasthan was conferred the Germany-based 2000 Nuclear-Free Future Solutions Award, for its remarkable work in training ordinary rural men and women in fabricating, installing, repairing and maintaining sophisticated solar energy lighting systems in cold and hot deserts and tribal indigenous.
8. S. Roy, "Voluntary Agencies in Rural Development—Their Role, Policy and Programmes", Indian Journal of Public Administration, Vol. 33, No. 3, pp. 454-64.
9. According to Anil Singh, Director, VANI, which is working to create a conducive environment for the smooth functioning of the NGO sector.
10. Anil Aggarwal, "Empower Civil Society', *Voluntary Action Pulse*, January 2000, p. 12.

4

Educational and Other Strategies of Non-Governmental Organisations

Any child in the age range of 5 to 15 years, who is doing labour, either paid or unpaid, and is kept working at any hour of the day, within or outside the family, is being deprived of the right to education. So all out-of-school children are child labourers in one form or another. All those NGOs that aim to promote education for children are seen to be indirectly helping in the eradication of the problem of child labour and therefore, fall under the purview of the present study.

The reason of laying emphasis to schooling is because education – compulsory primary education – is an important tool to tackle child labour. Historically, abolition of child labour was closely linked with the introduction of compulsory education. This was the experience of several countries described very vividly by Myron Weiner[1]. Introduction of compulsory primary education means that for at least a part of the day children would have to remain in school on a compulsory basis. It is argued that although education by itself will not eradicate child labour but it will reduce and discourage it. Child labour and compulsory education cannot co-exist. Employers will find child labour uneconomic if it is available for only half a day and if the working child becomes more visible by virtue of being a student. Despite this being the case, Indian government has not made headway towards universalisation of primary education. The policy makers have not paid due attention towards mass education. The popular view in India is that child labour is necessary for the well being of the poor when the state is unable to provide relief and thus, the abolition of child labour must await poverty alleviation. However, poverty has not prevented governments of other developing countries from expanding mass education or making primary education compulsory. Many countries of Africa with income levels lower than India have expanded mass education with impressive increases in literacy.[2]

The fact is that in our country universal primary education is yet to be given the importance it deserves. India spends just 1 per cent of its GDP on education of the weaker sections, almost 85 per cent of this 1 per cent goes to just 15 per cent people.[3] The Indian government has the capacity to make education compulsory but lacks the political leadership that is prepared to do what is necessary. And here lies the criticality of the role of non-governmental organisations. The NGOs not only have to make people understand about the role of education, but also to dispel the misconception that compulsory education means that children will not be allowed to work at all. Children in all societies which have introduced compulsory education have combined schooling with work, but the priority has been education first and work later and not the other way around.[4] This is precisely what most NGOs surveyed in Delhi were doing, providing non-formal schooling to children who work and also to out of school children who presently are not working, and who are very likely to be absorbed in the labour force sooner or later. This is not to say that NGOs in Delhi are not making any effort to raise awareness and consciousness among the masses and policy makers or are not conducting any release in rehabilitation activities for the release of child labourers. This will become clear in the description of the activities of the NGOs surveyed.

1. NGOs Study in Delhi

The researchers collected data from the following 17 NGOs during August – October, 1997:

> Angaja Foundation; Ankur; Bal Sahyog; Bandhua Mukti Morcha (BMM); Butterflies; Centre of Concern for Child Labour (CCFCL); Child Relief and You (CRY); Community Aid and Sponsorship Programme (CASP); Deepalaya; Delhi Brotherhood Social Development Society (DBS); Mobile Crèches; Prayas; Salaam Baalak Trust (SBT); South Asian Coalition on Child Servitude (SACCS); Street Survivors India (SSI); Vidya; and YWCA-Asha Project.

The Chairperson/General Secretary/Director of the concerned NGO were interviewed as to what their strategies are to deal with the problem of child labour, difficulties that they encounter in the course of their work, examples of what they consider as good work in this field, what are the shortcomings in tackling the problem and what are their future plans. Brochures, Annual Reports and other published literature were also collected from these NGOs and a few project sites were visited to have a better grasp of the strategies pursued by them.

All the 17 organisations studied were set up to cater to the children who have to wage a daily survival and who live amidst squalor and ignorance. Many of these organizations are working in the slums and providing non-formal education, health care and recreational opportunities to the slum children. In Delhi, most of the child labourers are found in the informal sector, i.e., on the roadside restaurants or *dhabas*, teashops, private houses (as domestic workers), vendors, car cleaners, rag pickers, porters or *coolies*, shoe-shiners, and so on. Organisations like, BMM and SACCS, with their regional offices in different parts of the country, are mainly engaged in release and rehabilitation of child labour in the sectors notorious for engaging child labour, e.g., carpet industry, matchstick-making industry, lock-making and pottery industries, etc.

In our study two organisations Ankur and Vidya were not directly involved in working for child labourers. They primarily deal with educating children of the slums, who may or may not be working. Since education is a powerful tool of eliminating child labour, these two organisations are playing a significant role towards elimination of child labour. Similar is the case with the organisations such as CASP, Angaja Foundation and Mobile Crèche, which are helping needy children and their families and thereby engaged in the protection of child labour. The organisations such as Butterflies and Delhi Brotherhood Society, that are working with street children, are in favour of a clear demarcation between child labour and street children on the plea that the situation of street children is entirely different from that of child labourers living in a family environment.

All the NGOs are engaged in sensitising the general public, government officials and politicians regarding the problem of child labour so that a new awareness about the rights of child workers is created. In doing so, they are also utilising print and electronic media such as Television and radio.

Out of all these NGOs, CRY is unique in terms of being a support organisation. It networks with other NGOs and individuals working for the rehabilitation and elimination of child labour and provides them financial and non-financial support. CRY is not an implementing agency, but only supports programmes and projects of like-minded organisations needing support. Its non-financial support to NGOs consists of providing training materials, access to information, developing communication materials, professional expertise and consultancy.

The NGOs surveyed have developed linkages with schools run by the Municipal Corporation of Delhi, the National Open School and government run vocational centres such as Shramik Vidyapeeth, Small Industries Service Institute and Industrial Training Institutes (ITI), so that their child beneficiaries get proper education and training. Linkages have also been established with institutions like All India Institute of Medical Sciences (AIIMS), Ranbaxy, Indian Cancer Society, TB Association for referral services and professional health care inputs.

In general, the research literature suggests that child labourers come from families with many children. Couples in poor households have more children, partly because child labour reduces the cost of having children. High fertility, in turn, is a vicious cycle. It increases the need for the income provided by child labour; it also reduces education levels of the future generations, thereby helping to ensure that future generations will have high fertility since parents' education is one of the most important determinants of fertility. It is, therefore, important that family planning should be an important complementary policy tool for child labour programmes. However, none of the organisations, except Angaja Foundation and SBT, include family planning programmes in their efforts to help working and street children.

2. Target Group

The target group of the NGOs studied are the children engaged in marginal economic activities e.g. market vendors/street hawkers, shoe shining, car parking, scavenging, and so on. The poor slum children who neither work nor go to the school and hence are potential child labour. Organisations like BMM and SACCS works for children of the rescued bonded labourers from the stone quarries. Both of these organisations are working for the release and rehabilitation of children working in industries such as carpet weaving, fireworks, lock making, etc., situated in various States.

The most common category of target group in the survey was of slum children, followed by street and working children and lastly by children engaged in industrial work.

3. Area of Operation

The survey reveals that geographic location-wise the offices of the NGOs surveyed are spread throughout the different parts of Delhi. In some cases, project sites and offices are located at different places. For instance, the offices of BMM and SACCS are in Delhi while their area of operation is throughout the country in regions where child labour is rampant. BMM has set up a school for children of slum areas of Garhi, South Delhi. SACCS on the other hand, has a Rehabilitation Centre at the north-eastern part of Delhi in Ibrahimpur. Asha Project and Mobile Crèches are projects that are not area-specific, they are mobile and covers all the parts of Delhi. Since CRY is a supporting organisation, its area of operation like BMM and SACCS is spread throughout the country, providing financial and non-financial support to development workers who need these resources to work with deprived children. The area of operation of the NGOs studied are illustrated in the table[5] as under:

Name of the NGO	*Area of operation within Delhi*
BMM	South Delhi Slum
SACCS	North-east Delhi (Ibrahimpur)
Deepalaya	South and Central Delhi (Slums of Chittaranjan Park, Sanjay Colony, Okhla Industrial area, Panchsheel Colony, Azadpur, Govindpur, Ramnagar
Prayas	West and South Delhi (Slums of Jahangirpuri, Patel Nagar, Kirti Nagar)
Asha Project	Mobile – throughout Delhi
Mobile Crèches	Mobile – at construction sites all over Delhi
SSI	Central Delhi (Slums of Motia Khan)

(*Contd.*)

(*Contd.*)

Name of the NGO	*Area of operation within Delhi*
SBT	Central Delhi (Paharganj, in and around the New Delhi Railway Station)
Angaja Foundation	South and Central Delhi (Slum areas)
DBS	East Delhi and Old Delhi (Slum areas of Jama Masjid, also at Interstate Bus Terminal, Hanuman Mandir and Red Fort)
CASP	South Delhi (Slums of Govindpuri)
CCCL	East Delhi
Bal Sahyog	West and Central Delhi (Resettlement colonies)
Ankur	South Delhi (Slum areas in R.K. Puram, Munirka)
Butterflies	Central Delhi

From the above table, it is clear that projects for slum children and street and working children exist in all parts of Delhi – North, West, East, South and Central. However, the concentration of projects are largely in the slums of South Delhi and Central Delhi, which are the places where the influx of migrants has been overwhelming, who come here seeking a better life, a job and home.

4. Philosophy and Aims

With regard to the philosophy, aims and objectives, three of the organisations namely Deepalaya, CASP and BMM are inspired by the ideals of equality and social justice. BMM under the influence of Arya Samaj movement for social reform does not only seeks to condemn child labour and proposes for its outright ban; but also strives for fairness and equality, regardless of caste, creed and gender. On the other hand, the mission of Deepalaya and CASP is to create an environment conducive for academic, physical, mental and social development of children. CASP's vision is of "a world in which children realise their full potential in societies, which respect people's rights and dignity". Deepalaya aims to establish "a new peaceful socio-economic, politico-cultural order which will help and enlighten communities to transform themselves into self-reliant, self-governed and exploitation free social structures that will foster a healthy and appropriate environment for the development of disadvantaged, especially the children".

The rest of the organisations studied profess to restore childhood back to the disadvantaged and working children. Prayas goes to the extent of saying that "the most fundamental right of a child, particularly the disadvantaged and neglected, is restoration of childhood". These organisations believe that the needs of care and protection, shelter and home, education and counselling, nutrition and health are fundamental to the child's existence. Organisations such as the SSI, Deepalaya, CASP and Ankur believe that work with children must be participatory in character. Just conducting charity nurtures a dependency complex among the beneficiaries. SSI holds the belief that "projects for street and working children have a self-sustaining future only if the child beneficiaries themselves become the resource persons to run these".

5. NGOs and Funding

Since the focus of the study is to find out what are the initiatives and interventions for protection and rehabilitation for child labour, undertaken by NGOs, only marginal attention has been paid to the funding aspect. The main sources of funding for these NGOs are the government and the foreign funding agencies. These include: Ministry for Social Welfare, Ministry of Human Resource Development, Directorate of Social Welfare (Delhi Administration), Delhi Social Welfare Advisory Board, International Labour Organisation, United Nations International Children and Education Fund, Save the Children's Fund, Canadian International Development Agency, British High Commission, OXFAM[6], Charities in U.K.[7] and PLAN International. The organisation Bal Sahyog, being funded by the Delhi Administration is running a Boat Club at the India Gate and the income derived from the Boat Club is utilised for the care and welfare of boys at Bal Sahyog Home and its various contact clubs.

Besides, almost all of these NGOs have sponsorship schemes through which to appeal to the community to sponsor a child's monthly or annual expenditure on education, nutrition, clothing and health care. They also have schemes of one time corpus donation[8], the income of which takes care of a child's needs for the lifetime. At the same time, the NGOs accept funds from the corporate houses and the public at large. A concession of tax exemption of the amount donated from the Income Tax under 80G and 35 AC is provided to the corporate bodies and those who have professional income. An 80G Certificate allows donors to deduct the contribution to charitable organisations from their income tax. At present, there is an incentive of 50 per cent tax deductibility under 80 G. Under Section 35 AC/80GGA one can avail of 100 per cent tax exemption. This tax benefit is available only for donations in cash.

The funding aspect in case of the organisations BMM and SBT has been discussed in chapters 5 and 6. Here, we would discuss briefly the unique effort of resource generation by two of the organisations, namely Deepalaya and CRY. Deepalaya established a 'Communication Division' in 1990, with the aim of raising funds at low cost within the country and to build a broad based domestic support to build public awareness through wide ranging participation in fund raising efforts. Some of the areas and strategies evolved by it during 1996-97 are:

- Placing donation boxes on the counters of leading chemists, shops, hotels, departmental stores, and ice cream parlours and garment shops. These have been sources of regular income and it also gives an opportunity for the organisation to communicate its mission and objectives to people at large through these chains of outlets.
- Shop-n-share, is an innovative fund raising venture which was launched with some of the leading retail outlets to help Deepalaya by means of a contribution of Rs. 2 from each customer per purchase.
- Airing TV Chat Shows and Radio programmes to sensitise people on the issue of child labour. People would donate generously for the cause if they were aware of the hardships of child labourers.

Coming to the organisation CRY, it has its own structure of fund raising activities. The Resource Generation function of CRY is divided into — Corporate Partnership and Individual Partnership. This is to provide its supporters (i.e. individuals who donate to its schemes and corporate houses who generally buy its cards and fund some of its projects) with more opportunities to participate in its work.

5.1 CRY's Fund Raising Schemes

The different fundraising schemes of CRY to which one can donate and thus reach out to the deprived children are as follow:

(a) *Child Sponsorship Scheme* — Where the donor's money goes to support the education and health of children in CRY supported projects all over India.
(b) *Child Development Fund* — This is the very foundation on which CRY stands. Thus, when support is extended to Child Development Fund, it ensures the stability of CRY's support to its project partners.
(c) *Helping Hand Scheme* — Helping Hand Scheme (HHS) focuses on creating a better future for disadvantaged children by sponsoring a child's education and other basic needs. Donations to HHS go to support activities which help in the all round development of the child. It involved airing an advertisement encouraging people to *'try giving once for a needy child and see the difference it can make'* in major satellite channels on the television. CRY has received overwhelming responses not only from people in India but also from people living in Bahrain, Dubai, Kuwait, Muscat, Abu Dhabi, Nepal and even from Holland.
(d) *Adopt-a-Project*: This scheme is targeted at corporate houses and organisations. Under this scheme organisations can fund either partially or entirely a CRY funded project of its interest. For instance, Kurd Consultancy selected 'Sharan', a project that runs primary schools, crèches, community organisation programmes etc., in the slums in West and South Delhi.[9] Kellogg's contributed Rs. 4,35,480 for 'Doorstep School', which runs education centres for children who work in fisheries in Sassoon Docks.[10]

CRY's Products: CRY markets its products for the benefit of the deprived children. These products include greeting cards, paintings, gift bags, presentation sets, desk calendars, scribble pads and telephone and address book.[11]

6. Initiatives for Child Labourers

On the basis of the survey of activities/strategies, adopted by the NGOs studied, the following typology has been arrived at:

Table 5.1 Types of Initiatives by the NGOs Surveyed

	Type of Activity	*Total No. of NGOs*
1.	Raid/Release/Rehabilitation of Child Labourers	2
2.	Provision of non-formal education and recreational opportunities	15
3.	Establishing Primary Education Centres	5
4.	Facilitating school attendance by providing food, clothing, books, waiver of school fees, admitting children in local schools	12
5.	Counselling and health care services	11
6.	Protective Measures such as providing gloves, sunglasses, I-cards to children to use in their work, forming credit-unions, cooperatives for child labourers	2
7.	Sponsorship programmes	7
8.	Establishing 'Shelter Homes' for street and working children	6
9.	Establishing vocational-cum-rehabilitation centres	3
10.	Sharing government responsibility like running its Children's Observation Home and Child Helpline Service	3
11.	Skill development activities and flexible schooling	14
12.	Income-generating activities for families or communities	4
13.	Other community development activities	8
14.	Documentation and publication	5
15.	Networking	11
16.	Conducting workshops/seminars on child labour issues	5
17.	Conducting campaigns, marches, demonstrations for mass sensitisation	6
18.	Financial and non-financial support to projects on child labour	1

6.1 Non-Formal Education and Recreational Activities Provisions

The provision of non-formal education (NFE) and recreational activities, designed to break the cycle of child labour and to help ensure their entry into schools, is the most common kind of activity undertaken by the NGOs surveyed. Such activities do not replace any income children forego, but have the aim of persuading children to reduce their hours of work or leave their work altogether. When implemented in a slum situation where there are no schools, these activities tend to prevent children from becoming child labourers. While the purpose of some organisations, like Deepalaya, Prayas, Angaja Foundation is to mainstream children into regular schools some other organisations like SBT and SSI, believe that the formal education system is inadequate to meet the educational needs of street and working children and hence there is the need to provide basic non-formal education tailored to suit the needs of such children.

According to SSI, the needs of street and working children are not just confined to non-formal education. They need support services tailored to meet their educational, nutritional, health and vocational needs. The SSI regards that rapidly increasing number of school dropouts is a sign of the irrelevance of the formal system. It does not, train children in employable skills. The organisation believes that there is an urgent need for evolving plans at the grassroots to address the needs of local communities.

To realise this need, SSI built up a low-cost school called "*Jagriti*", in the slums of Motia Khan (Central Delhi) in 1990, using wooden poles, bamboo frames and matting – much like the shanties that children lived in all their lives. From such modest beginnings with a single class of 25 children, "Jagriti School" has since grown and diversified into a campus of several low-cost buildings within the slum. It accommodates a programme of primary education in two shifts between 8 a.m. and 4 p.m., five days a week, benefiting 350 children mostly in the age group of 5-12 years. The majority are 7 to 12 years old, about half being girls. The organisation realises that personalised and non-formal teaching methods help children overcome the handicaps of formal schooling. For instance, even tiny girls, in the poor community, are burdened with the responsibility of taking care of younger siblings. The school allows such girl children to bring their younger siblings to the school.

The daily regimen of the school consists of a morning assembly of physical exercise and singing followed by a programme of functional literacy and social awareness in Hindi, as well as basic arithmetic. For the more advanced learners, there is a study of geography and history. Other activities for children include clay modelling or drawing, and theatre workshops to conduct a dialogue with the children on their day-to-day problems. This is done to instill an awareness of the world at large and their place within it.

The organisation Deepalaya has similar belief regarding education as the key to social transformation. The education pattern followed by Deepalaya is interactive in nature and aims to meet the varied needs of the community. It has the distinction of being accredited to National Open School[12] to get the students certified by the appropriate authorities in education and vocational training. The dynamic character of the learning programmes provides the appropriate environment for educating children outside conventional schools and colleges through a specially designed self-study programme.

Prayas on the other hand, considers NFE as its area of excellence. Prayas NFE programme is a three-year compiled course designed on BRAC (Bangladesh Rural Advancement Committee) model. In this programme, children are taught using the chart and card board method. They are provided with specially designed NFE books, a pair of uniforms, mid-day meal besides educational trips to museums and places of historical interest. The trips aims at providing an exposure to the outside world. After the completion of the three-year NFE course, those children, who want to continue studies are enrolled in the municipal corporation (MCD) schools through the mediation of Prayas which gets their birth-certificates (necessary for admission) made for them. Vocational training is provided to those children who are between 12-14 years of age. There is also a provision for admission into 'National Open Schools' and the 'Foundation Courses of Open Schools' to interested children.

The organisation Ankur also needs a special mention here. Ankur runs educational programmes with children in five slums of South Delhi. Ankur focuses on primary education. It seeks to understand the child's point of view vis-à-vis experience of education and initiates a dialogue between school-teachers and educational authorities and the slum children and their siblings and parents. It also networks with individuals and groups concerned about improvement of the education system. Instead of offering incentives to the children who come to study, as some other NGOs do, Ankur charges rupee one per month as a fee. It weaves in the curriculum issues of communalism, gender bias, housing rights, current issues, rising prices, and such other topics. Children are encouraged to talk on topical issues and are given assignments such as that of writing the history of their slum. The emphasis is on creativity rather than on rote learning.

The NFE package offered by the all NGOs surveyed is usually of 3 years duration after which children are encouraged admission in government schools. This is a serious flaw in the approach followed by the NGOs because the standard of education in the government schools is very low and whatever the children learn under the auspices of the NGOs are soon unlearnt in these schools. This points to the fact that to provide a secure and bright good future for children, the work of the NGOs needs to be supplemented with strengthening and improving the standard of education in government schools as well.

6.2 Flexible Schooling

The strategy of flexible schooling comprises of providing vocational training to children along with the non-formal education. School-work programmes allow children to go to school, e.g., in the morning, and work during the afternoon to earn some money. Schools have flexible hours to enable children to work and include for instance vocational training components in the curriculum to support the work. School-work programmes do not cause opportunity costs in the form of lost earnings. Most of the organisations surveyed, except BMM and SACCS, are positive in attitude towards them. These programmes do not eliminate child labour, instead seek to provide an alternative which helps build human capital through school, while reducing hours of work and allowing for the poor family's need for income at the same time. However, this approach is based on the understanding that poor children need to work to supplement the family's income and thus, in a way legitimises child labour.

Out of the 17 NGOs surveyed, 14 of them, as is evident from the table, emphasized the importance of adding vocational training in children's education. They rightly believe that education should have a vocational training component to enable the children to become self-reliant. Some of the commonly taught vocations are: candle-making, screen-printing, scooter-repairing, beauty care, cutting and tailoring, in-house electrical wiring, plumbing, detergent making, incense stick making, chalk making, clay-modelling, theatre arts[13], carpentry, welding, repairing of electrical gadgets, leather work, motor mechanics, computer courses, embroidery, book-binding and making of sweet boxes. Regular exhibitions are held by the NGOs to display and sell the items made by the children.

The NGOs, despite their avowedly progressive ideals, have been unable to shake off gender stereotyping of occupations. Training in carpentry, welding, motor mechanics, repairing electrical gadgets, in-house electrical wiring is still imparted to boys whereas embroidery, cutting and tailoring, screen-printing and the beauty care course are earmarked for girls.

The vocational training as provided by Bal Sahyog needs mention here. The training is provided in its Shelter Home for boys. The duration of the training is three years with simultaneous schooling upto 7th Standard. It also offers short-term course in book-binding and electronics. Vocational training is imparted by the trained personnel of the government of India through the Small Industries Service Institute (SISI). After the successful completion of the course, boys are awarded a certificate by the SISI. These certificates entitle them for admission to Industrial Training Institute (ITI) courses which allow the trainees to become highly skilled in specialized branches. The Delhi Administration reserves two seats for the trainees from Bal Sahyog.

Although, NGOs are able to cite only a few examples of children who have benefited from their training programmes, it is clear however, that the children do acquire employable skills through such programmes.

6.3 Opening Primary Education Centres or Model Schools

Although, all the organisations surveyed believe in the need for providing education for child labourers, most of them are satisfied with the provision of short-term non-formal education. Only five of them, viz., Deepalaya, SACCS, SSI, DBS and Bal Sahyog make special efforts to educate the child workers and street children through the schools established by them.

Some of the schools, primary as well as secondary, established by Deepalaya in South Delhi slums include: (a) Deepalaya School at Sanjay Colony; (b) Ramditi Jr. Narang Deepalaya Schools; and (c) Deepalaya School-Govindpuri. These schools provide "broad-based education that combines extra-curricular activities with academic inputs, to ensure holistic development of the child". The Deepalaya School at Govindpuri is its latest initiative. Its location is such that it is accessible to nearly nine surrounding slum clusters of South Delhi, with a population of over fifty five thousand. It is envisaged as the main school for higher and comprehensive learning in academic and in vocational streams.

SACCS, with the objective of universal primary education, is running 20 primary schools in different states from where it has released child labourers. These schools are catering to the educational needs of those child labourers for whom education was otherwise a distant dream.

It is worthwhile to mention here about the Bal Sahyog Middle School, which provides schooling upto the 8th standard. The school is duly recognised by the Directorate of Education. After completion of schooling till 8th standard, children are given full assistance for enrolment to the National Open Schools.

The organisation Butterflies that works with the street children is against the concept of setting up of alternative education centres. As the Director of Butterflies puts it, "there is no need to set up new schools, the educational standard of the already existing Municipal Schools should be improved and people should be mobilised to do that".

6.4 Providing Incentive to Increase School Attendance

Of the 17 NGOs surveyed, 12 are engaged in providing educational support to children by paying for their books, notepads and pencils, uniforms, shoes, transport, etc.[15] The idea is to ensure that the children stay on in school and reduce the drop-out rate and absenteeism. The organisations like Prayas and SSI serves hot cooked meal at the school to ensure that working children eat nutritious food at least once a day.

BMM goes to the extent of demanding from the government that each school going child be given 1 kg of cereal for each schooling day both as an incentive and as a measure of food security for their poor families.

Such financial support to children runs the risk of misuse; there are adequate incentives for unscrupulous people to siphon off the funds in a variety of ways. For instance, in-kind payments of school materials such as clothing or pads and pencils may be sold instead of being used by the child designed to attend school. As such, this intervention is to be used with caution by NGOs working for promoting education among children.

6.5 Counselling and Health Care

Counselling and health care are two important needs of the child labourers or slum children. Children who have been burdened at an early stage to work, develop a low esteem about themselves and develop a variety of complexes. Their self-confidence is also low. They need to be counselled on their psychological problems. Counselling helps them to understand life, the environment and human dynamics and equips them with coping skills. Most of the NGOs surveyed, 11 out of 17 of them, realise the psychological needs of working children and have employed qualified psychologists for the purpose.

As working children live under unsanitary conditions they suffer from numerous ailments and NGOs working for such children organise regular health check-ups and provide for their treatment and hospitalisation. They have also established referral linkages with the local health clinics run by the MCD and the local hospitals so that children can be taken to these hospitals in case of health emergencies.

The organisation Prayas possess three Medical Mobile Vans, which takes a round of all of its 9 slum centres to attend to the health needs of the children. It also has an indoor facility – a Nursing Home with 10 beds and a regular doctor to deal with serious medical problems. Some specialists in the field of medicines, also serve the organisation on voluntary basis. Prayas is networking with other NGOs in running its health programme.

Although such health programmes are laudable, they are only curative and are ineffective in preventing ailments by improving their environment.

6.6 Protective Measures

Safety training and safety equipments are provided to the working children to minimise occupational hazards. Two of the NGOs surveyed viz., DBS and Butterflies were found to have adopted this strategy. Both these organisations work for street and working children. DBS tries to regulate the working conditions of such children. For instance, the organisation provides sunglasses and gloves to the rag-picker children, and has formed a cooperative for them so that they may work in a systematic, organised and hygienic way. Similarly, Butterflies has started a savings scheme and a credit union to mobilise and empower child workers. Since street children are highly mobile and keep migrating from one city to the other, Butterflies gives identity cards to its child beneficiaries who ask for it. With these Identity Cards, these children feel secure, safe and have a sense of belonging to the organisation.

The ideology behind such protective measures is that 'child labour is a necessary evil', hence children's working conditions have to be regulated. However, such a strategy only serves to ameliorate the problem besides legalising child labour.

6.7 Sponsorship Programme

Sponsorship programme is like a self-financing scheme; it aims to fulfill the needs of education, health and recreation of working children through mobilising community's financial resources. In this scheme, a sponsor virtually adopts a child by paying for the upkeep of the child and his/her health and educational needs. In order to attract big businessmen and corporate houses, the donations are exempted from income tax. The motivating philosophy behind sponsorship ventures as elaborated by the organisation Prayas is as under:

> Biological parenthood does not automatically confer the desire, skill and capacity to care for children, but the children should not be separated from their parents. Sponsorship is the only alternative to care for such children by allowing the transfer of responsibilities and privileges of parenting from the biological parents to God-parents.[16]

NGOs try to create a bond between the child and his/her sponsor by encouraging them to correspond through letters and cards, by the exchange of gifts on special occasions and festivals, and through arranging meetings between them at regular intervals.

Thus, the monetary relationship between the child and his/her sponsor is sought to be converted in an intimate relationship, based on love and affection. The procedure of sending money to the child is tried to be strengthened by the ties of love and affection.

The sponsorship programme is a unique way of mobilising local resources for the betterment of children. However, not many people come forward to sponsor a child through NGOs. The sponsorship scheme is not very successful since people till now are suspicious of the NGO sector and are hard to be convinced that their money will be utilised for the stated purpose.

6.8 Establishing Shelter Homes

In order to make available a secure space where street and working children can live, study, play and enjoy their childhood, some NGOs have attempted to provide institutional care in the form of Shelter Homes. In the absence of these Homes, street and working children are forced to spend their nights on pavements or railway station platforms or any public place or open space, where they not only have to brave the harsh weather conditions but also are vulnerable to sexual harassment. These shelter homes are of several types, as given below:

(a) 24 Hour Drop-in-Shelter, where children can drop in any time of the day or night, avail bathing and toilet facilities, take rest or sleep at night. However, certain formalities are required to be fulfilled in order to the use of such shelters. For instance, the boys coming to the 24 hour Drop-in-Shelter are observed for one month. And only after being found to be regular visitors, that they are admitted in the Shelter. Their educational and medical need is taken care of. The boys who wish to study further are helped in getting admitted to formal schools. Vocational training is also imparted to the boys and are further helped in job placement.

(b) *Shelter Homes*: These are just like homes for shelterless working children. Like a home, it gives freedom as well as has regulations imposed to the children dwelling here. There are set timings for each activity and inmates of the Shelter Homes have to strictly abide by them. Here complete care of children, right from their nutrition and education to their proper upbringing is taken.

(c) *Night Shelter*: As the name suggests, the purpose of Night Shelter is to provide shelter to children with basic facilities at night. It runs from dusk to dawn. Some organisations like DBS have both a Shelter Home and a Night Shelter. Briefly, we would discuss here about the DBS Night Shelter. DBS Night Shelter is for those children who do not want to come to the Home since they do not like its disciplined life. It is open from 6 p.m. to 10 a.m. Its daily routine includes bathing, washing, cleaning of the room, recreation, sports, study and dinner. Here, children are also given orientation for 3 hours, in which they are taught social education, literacy and are provided recreational facilities.

Such 'homes away from homes' are a need for shelterless working children who run away from their homes due to various reasons and are in extremely vulnerable situations.

However, the strategy of providing shelter homes has certain short comings. NGOs may give the best help within the Institution/Homes to the street and working children, but when children come out they are sent out of these closed shelters in the mainstream society, they may feel totally out of place, without any protection and without any place to turn to. Hence, NGOs must make efforts to help such children to settle down in life. The Drop-in-Shelters and Night Shelters, which allow children to work outside and avail of the basic facilities from the shelters, tend to legitimise child labour. Another drawback of the strategy of Shelter Homes is that such "institutional care" needs much financial investment for setting them up, and therefore, it is not economically viable to set up such Homes all over the country. Also, the above account leads us to conclude that there exists a dilemma of sorts – either free the children from work and 'protect' them or allow them to work and support them to achieve a better quality of life.

6.9 Raid and Rescue Operations

Raid and rescue operations are the main strategies adopted by the "radical" NGOs like BMM and SACCS. These activities aim to eliminate child labour from the country. The NGOs adopting this strategy conduct raids in whichever industries or operations, from where they get information from local populace and release/rescue the working children or bonded children below the age of 14 years working in such occupations. In these operations, the assistance of judiciary, police and the local officials is also sought. How BMM conducts raids to rescue child labourers has been described in chapter 5. Here, mention would be made of the raid and rescue operations conducted by SACCS.

SACCS activists try to make their presence felt in areas notorious for the practice of child labour through consistent propaganda. After winning over the confidence of the local population, the relatives of the child are informed. The possibilities of the rescue operations are then worked out in association with the legal bodies/individuals. Often the help of the government machinery is also sought in the process. Eventually, efforts are made to provide the rehabilitatory benefits entitled to them under the various governmental schemes.

Although rehabilitation is a very important component of release and rescue operations, due to the governmental apathy and insufficient follow-up by the concerned NGOs, the released workers soon join the labour market.

6.10 Establishing Vocational-cum-Rehabilitation Centres

Realising the fact that rescue loses its value without proper rehabilitation, some of the NGOs engaged in releasing children from bondage and from hazardous and non-hazardous occupations, realise the need for establishing 'rehabilitation centres'. The aim of such centres is to "mitigate the battered feeling of child labourers and provide them with basic education and vocational training along with making them aware of their rights and obligations". In this context the "Mukti *Ashram*" set by SACCS needs mention. Established in 1991 for the freed child labourers, this transitory vocational-cum-rehabilitation centre has an intake capacity of 60 trainees at a time. The entire cost, right from bringing these trainees from their villages, provision of food, accommodation, training and returning them back home is borne by the *Ashram*. The children receive basic literacy, hygiene and health care, social training and vocational training in different trades and crafts. SACCS proudly says "most of the trainees become economically independent in their native villages, besides helping the community to unite and struggle for their rights".

Such centres are need of the hour but they cater to only a miniscule population of freed child labourers. At the same time, they require the mobilisation of huge amounts of financial resources.

As long as children continue to be exploited and abused, whether in hazardous industries, in menial and degrading jobs, as bonded labour or as domestic help – such rehabilitative programmes can succeed only in a few cases.

6.11 Sharing Responsibility with the Government

This is a unique attempt of partnership between the government and NGOs. The government invites the NGOs to manage its badly managed Observation Homes or to involve them in operating the toll-free telephonic child helpline service for children in distress. For instance, Prayas and SBT have been given to manage Observation Homes for Destitute or Juvenile children. Similarly, SBT, Prayas and DBS are operating the child helpline service.[17]

Prayas took over the non-custodial function of the government-run-custodial home on 1st October 1996 and entered into collaboration with the Government of Delhi in taking care of neglected juveniles. On 1st April 1997, it took over even the custodial function as a pilot project in Delhi. The initiatives that are being undertaken in the Juvenile Homes include – non-formal education for 200 children, vocational training, nutrition, and provision of bedding, clothing and shelter, counselling, regular health check-ups and referral services.

The idea behind such a partnership between government and NGOs is that NGOs are more sensitive to children and can be more effective in handling children.

6.12 Income-Generating Activities for Families or Communities

Income-generating activities for families and communities include support for micro-enterprises, credit schemes and employment training for mothers and or/fathers. They are designed to improve the economic situation of families and communities to reduce the family's reliance on child labour. Although an important activity, only four out of the seventeen NGOs studied are engaged in such activities. These NGOs include Deepalaya, Bal Sahyog, SSI and CASP.

Deepalaya is running different types of skill enhancement and income generation programmes to help the slum dwellers augment their meagre incomes and manage their resources well. Monetary assistance is also given to set up business ventures and necessary market tie-ups are made available. The trade/ventures in which the beneficiaries are trained are – chalk making units, petty trading and micro-enterprises, embroidery and handicraft units. The NGO has also established corporate linkages to find jobs for the personnel who have successfully undergone training.

On a smaller scale, Bal Sahyog, CASP and SSI are also attempting such a programme. While SSI has started an evening adult literacy-cum-savings cooperative, Bal Sahyog provides interest free loans to families of the child labourers to make them self-supporting.

In initiating such activities, questions such as who to target and how, what kind of training to provide in connection with income-generating activities; and how to ensure cost-effectiveness, need to be raised. Regarding cost-effectiveness, income-generating activities are clearly not designed to be welfare schemes, but to give families the tools and skills to escape from poverty. Therefore, when successful, they have a sustainable impact on the whole group of people and not just the targeted child.

6.13 Other Community Development Activities

Community development programmes are often comprehensive including other activities besides income-generation. They are aimed at the introduction of some new idea – be it girls' education, limiting the size of the family, treating girls and boys equally, teaching people to keep their slums neat and clean, helping the community to become self-reliant and slum dwellers in getting basic necessities, like drinking water and toilets.

Any intervention for child labourers could succeed only if it focuses on the environment in which these children live. Communities have to be helped to develop the means, abilities and motivations necessary to meet their own needs. The ultimate aim of community building programmes is to build strong, cohesive communities capable of achieving self-sufficiency. In this regard, CASP through its community based organisations (CBOs) tries to give extensive training to the people so that they can participate in the development process. CASP considers its success in being able to pull out of the community after the community takes charge of the project.

Similarly, the objective of Deepalaya is to make its CBOs self-reliant, self-managed and self-sufficient. Its CBOs are nurtured with women trained to play an active role in decision-making bodies. Special programmes for their active participation is organised. Girl child projects, skill training units, thrift and credit for women, mother and child care centres are examples of some of the projects it has taken up. Deepalaya, too adopts the approach of phasing-out of the projects and the experience has been encouraging.

Another important community welfare activity is that of family planning programme being run by Angaja Foundation and SBT. Angaja believes that it is important to curtail the number of children being born to parents already overburdened with looking after many others in the family, since fewer children means a better living standard. Angaja has, therefore, undertaken the family planning intervention among the community.

Community building programmes have long gestation periods because the kind of communities that are attempted to be built require heightened awareness and a spirit of participation, which is not easy to find especially in urban settings.

6.14 Documentation and Publication

Research, documentation and publication of news items, articles and material on major issues relating to child labour is conducted by some of the NGOs, viz., SACCS, Prayas, CRY, CCFCL and Butterflies. In order to promote social awareness on child labour issues, CCFCL, under the Human Rights Education Programme, sends out a monthly letter to intellectuals, concerned citizens, doctors, lawyers, engineers, businessmen, women executives, media personalities, policy-implementers, trade-unions, environmentalists, feminists, policy makers and social activists.

On the other hand, SACCS, through its publications, 'Break the Chains: Save Childhood', 'Rugmark: A Brief Resume of Concept to Reality', and its regular reports and pamphlets aims to dispel misconceptions relating to child labour and to develop a clear and correct perspective among the masses.

SACCS also undertakes research on the problem of child labour, which forms an integral part of its activity. It has been undertaking surveys and research work on other aspects of the problem.

CCFCL undertakes action research to collect micro-level information on the situation of child workers in various occupations and to create public opinion through public education programmes especially against the exploitation of girl children, children in hazardous occupations, child prostitutes and street children.

CRY has a Documentation Centre at Mumbai. The Centre collects information on child labour and shares the same with other organisations and individuals working on the issue in order to build a common platform. CRY also encourages other individuals and organisations to set up regional documentation centres to disseminate information to the public.

Research and documentation as well as publication are important activities. Apart from publicising the issue of the child labourer, it highlights the magnitude of the problem and the varieties of ways in which the practice of child labour perpetuates so that appropriate strategies for the elimination of child labour could be evolved. It tends to explore various aspects of child labour. However, documentation and publication on child labour has limited value in a country where half of the population is illiterate.

6.15 Campaigns/Marches/Demonstrations/Mass Sensitisation

The gravity of the problem of child labour may be publicised in the masses in a wider way and they may be mobilised through campaigns, marches and demonstrations. Six organisations – BMM, SACCS, CRY, Butterflies, CCFCL and Ankur – are engaged in one or the other of such activities. Two of the organisations studied, viz., BMM and SACCS, are also engaged in direct action by bringing pressure on the police to carry out raids and rescue operations as well. For instance, SACCS has been organising a number of marches to raise the awareness of the masses on the issue of child labour and enlist their support. It has organised several marches over the years, some of which are:

- A 1,500 k.m. long march from Bihar to New Delhi in 1993.
- 'Bharat Yatra', covering a distance of 5,000 kms. from Kanyakumari to Delhi in 1994.
- 'Foot March' in child labour pockets of Delhi in 1995.
- A 1,600 kms. long Child Labour Elimination March from Calcutta to Kathmandu in 1996.
- 'Mukti Rath Yatra' which aims at sensitising the masses against the evils of child labour in the various child labour prone areas through street plays, songs, dramas, etc.
- 'Global March against Child Labour' was organised in 1998 in collaboration with several like-minded organisations from around the world with the aim of placing the problem of child labour on the top of the world's agenda.

SACCS has launched various campaigns at national as well as international levels to sensitise various sections of society about the gravity of the problem and to demand concrete action to solve it. Some of the campaigns are:

Campaigns at the International Level: SACCS participates in various international fora, UN hearings etc., to draw global attention towards the problem of child labour in the South Asian region and the deplorable conditions of children in servitude. SACCS launched a Global Campaign, 'the carpet consumers awareness campaign' to highlight the plight of child labourers in carpet weaving. SACCS has been supported in this movement by organisations such as 'Bread for the World', 'Terre Des Hommes', Miserior' and German Trade Unions. Together with representatives of carpet industry, Indo-German Export Promotion Programmes (IGEP – a trade promotion organisation), UNICEF, carpet manufacturers (who do not employ children), NGOs, a certification system, named Rugmark Foundation, was developed to certify carpets made without the use of child labour.

The Rugmark Foundation: The Rugmark Foundation (RMF) was registered on 5 September 1994 as a private limited company under section 25 of the Indian Companies Act of 1956. The RMF is a non-commercial, independent, international and professional body with legal power to verify, inspect, monitor and subsequently affix a trade mark label, that is Rugmark logo, to the carpets which are not made by children. The Rugmark label on the carpets provides the importers and consumers a visual guarantee that these carpets are manufactured without child labour. Any carpet manufacturer/exporter who voluntarily agrees to produce carpets free of child labour can apply for critical inspections and issue of licence from RMF. The cardinal criterion is that the manufacturer/exporter should employ only adult labour for the manufacture of his product. His workplace will be liable for inspections at any time. The firm will apply Rugmark Foundation along with the fees for the issue of licence. Once the Foundation is satisfied that the applicant has fulfilled all the required conditions after inspections and scrutiny, a licence agreement is made out and this would hold legally. After obtaining the licence, the manufacturer/exporter is free to use the Rugmark label in his carpet. To ensure that child labour is not used, there are regular and frequent inspections. The certification criteria covers the following:

- That the applicant is a bonafide dealer, manufacturer or exporter of carpets.
- That the applicant agrees to remove child labour, if any, from his production unit from the date of application.
- That the applicant has furnished an updated list of all the looms, loom owners and other allied work place related to carpet manufacturing. The loom units should have been registered with Carpet Export Promotion Council.
- That the applicant shall certify about the correctness of the list and intimate the RMF in the event of any change. Updating should be done every 6 months to facilitate the inspection team.
- That the applicant shall certify that the carpets submitted for inspection are not produced by children (under 14 years of age).

Another condition that needs to be fulfilled is declaration that applicant will not pay less than the official minimum wages to the loom owners. In turn the loom owner has to submit an affidavit to the applicant indicating that no child is employed in his workplace and that all the employees are being paid as per minimum wages declared by the Government.

SACCS is presently making further attempts to replicate this certification system in other industries.

Campaigns at the National Level

(a) *School Campaign*: In order to motivate the young minds against the evil of child labour, SACCS organises competitions (essay writing, painting, plays, songs and debates in schools) on the topic of child labour. This gives an opportunity to the children to express their views on the prevalence of child labour.

(b) *Advocacy with Political Parties*: The main aim of advocacy is to persuade the political parties to include the issue of eliminating child labour, and imparting free, compulsory education in their election manifestoes.

(c) *Campaign for Universal Primary Education*: SACCS realises the importance of education as a liberating force. Hence, it has launched a nationwide campaign, 'Liberation for Education, Education for Liberation'. This is primarily to pressurise the government to take requisite steps to achieve the goal of universal primary education.

(d) *Domestic Consumer Boycott Campaign*: SACCS organises consumer boycott campaigns from time to time, against industries and establishments employing child labour such as glass and bangles produced in Firozabad (Uttar Pradesh), fireworks of Sivakasi (Tamil Nadu), tea shops, restaurants, garages, etc. The purview of such campaigns is not restricted to industries alone, but also extends to the households where in people are motivated to boycott the hospitality of such households which employ children as domestic servants.

Despite these attempts made by SACCS and certain other NGOs the practice of child labour persists with impunity. This calls for campaigning and demonstrating much more vigorously so as to increase awareness and consciousness among the general public and the policy makers against the practice of child labour.

6.16 Conducting Workshops and Seminars

Such activities are intended to create awareness about the various aspects of the problem of child labour. Out of the 17 NGOs studied, 5 of them, viz., SACCS, BMM, CCFCL, Butterflies and Ankur are engaged in such kind of activities. For instance, SACCS has been organising workshops and seminars with participants from various national and international organisations such as ILO, UNICEF, National Human Rights Commission (NHRC), and the like, with the aim of building a network among the various organisations. These apart from creating awareness about the various aspects of the problem of child labour, also foster experience sharing and acts as a platform to evolve strategies to effectively deal with the problem.

The strategies of awareness raising by publication, documentation, campaigns, demonstration, seminars and workshops are all preventive in nature. In the context of resource raising, preventive programmes usually face many problems. The concern for accountability poses a major hurdle in implementing programmes of a preventive nature mainly because the yard sticks for assessing the effectiveness of such programmes not only tend to be invisible but also are not easy to determine. Besides, it is usually more difficult to make a community understand the value of preventive programmes.

6.17 Networking

Networking is another crucial and effective activity. Networking with other like-minded organisations fosters experience sharing and acts as a platform to evolve strategies to effectively deal with the problem. Networking among organisations strengthens their position in influencing public opinion and finally changing government policy in favour of protecting the rights of children. A majority of NGOs surveyed, 11 out of 17 viz., BMM, SBT, Ankur, Bal Sahyog, CCFCL, DBS, CRY, Prayas, SACCS and Deepalaya are claimed to be networking with other organisations engaged in the elimination of child labour, protection of children and rehabilitation of the freed child labour. However, there are few forums where these NGOs meet. Also, the mutual cooperation, which is necessary in such an activity, is missing and is replaced by competition among the organisations, hence networking is not successful and does not serve the intended purpose.

6.18 Financial and Non-Financial Support to Individuals and Organisations

This is basically an intervention of the organisation CRY, which is a support organisation. CRY acts as a link between people who have resources of money, skills, materials or time and development workers who need these resources to work with deprived children.

CRY reaches children through the Programme Support Division by giving support, which is both in terms of financial as well as non-financial to projects, resource centres, and fellowships and by networking. Here, it is imperative to understand a little about financial and non-financial support provided by CRY.

Under the financial support activity of CRY funds to the projects are channelised by the Programme Support Division to the small NGOs for the implementation of their projects and to cover their administrative costs. Coming now to the non-financial support provided by CRY, which aims to enhance the quality of its partner's work with children, such support activities include the following:

(a) Training of project personnel in the critical areas of education, health, project and financial management, income generation programmes and organisational development.
(b) Giving on-going professional guidance in the areas of project planning, monitoring and evaluation as well as constant moral support and encouragement.
(c) Creating communication material such as brochures, documentation of their successful methodologies, etc. to help professionals and NGOs devoted to the protection of children.
(d) Encouraging networking between projects, so that projects not only learn from each other's experiences but also work together on larger issues.
(e) Providing material support like educational materials, toys, clothes, etc., from the Material Bank in Delhi, for which a nominal community contribution is collected.
(f) Disseminating relevant information on new techniques and

methodologies with regard to children's issues from the documentation centre based in Mumbai.

CRY also supports the following activities through its Programme Support Division (PSD):

1. *Projects*: CRY supports small struggling and medium sized projects. Every project supported by CRY is carefully selected, monitored and evaluated by the PSD. CRY supports projects financially, as well as provides non-financial support in terms of training, materials, information, developing communication materials, professional expertise, consultancy and networking opportunities. The objective is to improve the quality of the programmes/ projects provided to the community. CRY ensures through its monitoring systems, that the money is well spent and impacts the lives of children. Priority is given in the areas of education, health, vocational training, income generation and community development.
   For instance, the M.V. Foundation is being supported by CRY since 1988. It has been providing financial as well as crucial non-financial assistance, such as training of project staff in capacity building, effective communication and play way method of teaching; information support, especially about funding agencies; professional inputs for consolidation and planning for documentation as well as inputs on financial management.
2. *Resource Centres*: CRY supports Resource Centres that have developed, or are likely to develop, expertise in areas which would enhance the quality of child focused development. These Resource Centres serve as a guide to the projects and individuals supported by CRY as well as non-CRY supported initiatives through the development of innovative model teaching methods, materials and training programmes. Priority is given to Resource Centres working in the areas of education and health.
3. *Fellowships*: CRY introduced the Rippan Kapur Fellowship Programme (in memory of its founder) in 1994 to encourage more and more people to take up or remain in child development as a career.

The underlying philosophy behind CRY is the belief that individuals can make a difference in changing our unjust social structure. CRY, too, was an individual initiative, set up by Rippan Kapur — a dreamer with the cause of children in his heart. India needs many more people to work in the field of social development. However, the lack of financial security and moral encouragement are often the two obstacles preventing individuals to pursue social work.

CRY awards Fellowships to individuals all over India who are working with children. Women and individuals working in rural areas and on the issue of child labour and child prostitution are given special consideration.

The Fellowships enable them to concentrate completely on the task at hand without having to worry about personal finances.

Ultimately the success of CRY is linked with the success of its partners in transforming the lives of children.

The kind of support function undertaken by CRY needs huge amount of financial resources and professional expertise. CRY has developed its own strategy of fundraising for meeting the cost. But NGOs cannot undertake this kind of function on a large scale, since they have limited money and manpower. It should be the government that ought to be performing this role of supporting well-intentioned voluntary effort.

7. Future Plans

When asked regarding the initiatives they would like to undertake in future if funds were available to them, almost all the 17 NGOs surveyed, except Ankur, expressed to either carry out further their existing work on a much larger scale or initiate some new activities such as programmes on awareness generation, research on child labour[18] and carry out other rehabilitative works. According to Ankur, funds are not going to make any difference to the existing scenario unless there is also a political will, commitment and a vision.[19]

Some interesting and noteworthy future plans informed by the organisations deserve mention. For instance, Deepalaya plans to have a Deepalaya Gram Complex, which is envisaged to provide services to 3000 street and working children in a span of 10 years. According to the Chairperson of Deepalaya, Deepalaya would establish a chain of education centres with life-education and basic education as components.

SSI on the other hand, is engaged in buying 30 acres of land in a village, out of which, it would use 2 acres of land for its project-site and use the remaining 28 acres land for bamboo plantation. The income thereby from the plantation would be utilised for the projects so that the organisation becomes self-sufficient and self-sustaining.

DBS informed of its current initiative of having undertaken a research study on children working in '*dhabas*' (roadside eating-places). If funds are available to them, it would like to conduct a second-phase of the study wherein efforts would be made to generate public awareness within a 5-km radius of the '*dhaba*' in order to mobilise adults against the evil consequences of child labour. The awareness generation campaign is targeted towards the middle classes (who employ children as domestic servants), the public sector, shops and schools, etc.

CASP with the availability of funds intended to conduct more programmes in the nature of income-generation activities, and also to initiate "open schools" and "recreation rooms" for child workers.

On the other hand, CCFCL planned to make a comparative study of child labour in India and China. China is the only country, which is comparable to India in terms of its size and population. CCFCL would investigate how China has tackled the problem of child labour, what are its policies and how it has implemented them. This research would be an action-oriented one since CCFCL would like to follow-up its research into the policies and implementation of laws/programmes/projects of China in the field of child labour, with the aim of propagating of such policies in India.

8. Best Strategies Identified by NGOs

The NGO heads were also asked about what they considered some of the best examples of work in the field of child labour. Their opinions regarding some of the best practices in the field of child labour are summed up as follows:

1. SACCS and BMM, which advocate for a complete ban on child labour and are engaged in releasing and rehabilitating

children out of the work force, consider the advocacy approach for a total ban on child labour and of rehabilitating the existing child labourers, as the best example of work for child labour.[20]

2. Prayas[21] , Angaja Foundation, Delhi Brotherhood Society (DBS), Bal Sahyog, considers the package of non-formal education along with vocational training, nutrition, health care, reaching out to the children and motivating them away from work, as good and replicable strategy.
3. The organisation Vidya considers the kind of awareness generation on child labour created by CRY through its advertisement campaign as good work in the field of child labour.
4. Deepalaya considers the strategy of providing support services to the children who have to work, as being done by Butterflies, DBS, Prayas, SBT and Deepalaya itself, as the best.
5. According to the Street Survivors India, the best practice of work with children is that which involves children in formulating plans for themselves instead of the organisation deciding on what is right for the children.
6. Butterflies and CASP believe in dealing with the issue of child labour holistically with a multi-pronged approach.
7. According to SACCS, the awareness generation campaign at the global level, which has resulted into the Rugmark Foundation, is a good example of work in the field of children.

9. Difficulties Faced

The NGOs surveyed listed the following difficulties encountered by them in working in the field of child labour.

1. One of the major difficulties faced by the NGOs is that they are not clear on the definition of child labour. There is still a lot of ambiguity regarding who constitutes child labour[22] and children under what age groups constitutes child labour.
2. The pessimistic approach of the government that "child labour is viewed as a necessary evil", hampers the work of those NGOs who advocates for the total elimination of child labour

without having to wait for the economic development to take place since it is the child labour which is the cause for poverty and not the other way around. At the same time, there is an atmosphere of general apathy among people. They do not accept child labour as a social problem. The NGOs feel that unless the mindset of the common people about the issue of child labour is changed, any work in this regard will not be successful.

3. The prevailing legislative environment, too pose a problem. There is no comprehensive Act that outrightly bans child labour of any kind. The most latest law on child labour, which is the 1986 Act on the Protection and Regulation of Child Labour has not been revised (as demanded by the NGOs) till now.
4. Another problem encountered by the NGOs is that of improper implementation of the existing laws on child labour due to corrupt and inefficient enforcement agency. There is a lack of political and administrative will because of the nexus between employers, politicians and bureaucrats, which makes it easy for employers of child labourers to bribe the enforcing authorities for letting the child to work. Also there is a vested interest in employing children for the employers, since children can be coaxed, can be made to work for meagre sums, which prompts the employers to engage children into work. And thus, the problem perpetuates.
5. NGOs also complain of the failure by the government to understand interventions being carried out by them to combat the evil of child labour. At the same time, the government adopts a non-participatory approach and does not invite the NGOs at the policy planning stage.
6. For the NGOs, there is insufficient information dissemination on the best strategies or examples of work being done for the prevention of child labour, because of not being able to participate in major international forums where there could be an exchange of views and experiences.
7. The prevailing atmosphere of insensitivity towards the rights and needs of the working children by police, employers, government officials, social workers and the general public,

especially the middle classes, hampers the work of NGOs. NGOs that are working with street children face problems due to the unsympathetic attitude of the police officials. Police harass these children; beat them up, and charge them for crimes, which they have not committed. When the street educators and other staff intervene, police personnel are not only rude and uncooperative but also sometimes keep the intervening NGO staff in its custody for no genuine reasons.

8. Illiteracy is a major problem encountered by the NGOs working in the field of child labour. As the parents are uneducated they do not understand the value of education for their children and thus it is difficult for the NGOs to motivate people to send their children to school, thereby promoting the vicious cycle of child labour.
9. Proper rehabilitation of child labour is a difficult task and it is also not a part of the government-run-programmes. There is also the difficulty of not being able to give a viable atmosphere to the children after they complete their education and training from the educational-cum-vocational centres operated by NGOs. The level of literacy provided by the NGOs are not recognised by the Government which demands Matriculation or Intermediate Certificates for its Diploma Courses in different vocations.
10. There is also a lack of efficient, committed and humane social workers as human resources in the NGO sector. There is more of a career orientation, people come only for jobs and on getting better opportunities they leave the organisation.
11. A major problem faced by the NGOs is that of insufficient funding. There is irregularity and red tapism in the release of funds by the government. Also the funding agencies gives funds for a short period; as a result the NGOs work in an atmosphere of uncertainty about the continuation of their projects.
12. For organisations which are based in slums, there are difficulties of surviving in a slum environment since such organisations have to pay for those social workers who have come before them and made false promises to the community. The General Secretary of Street Survivors India, summed up these difficulties in the following words: "When we work

here and gain people's confidence, the innocent people, who have till now been living under constant fear, feel that now they have at least somebody who can listen to them and fight for them. By getting involved in people's problems, with the real life issues, we come face to face with anti-social elements of the slums". In this kind of a tussle with the anti-social elements, the school set up at the slum by SSI has been demolished twice.

13. The organisations working with the street children and operating at the street level have the problem of invisibility. For instance, Butterflies do not have Shelter Homes where institutional care could be provided. It works at the grassroot level and therefore their operation sites are inaccessible to its activities. There are fewer funding agencies to fund such projects.
14. At the same time, very low priority is given to street children by the government. Street children are most affected from the environment, in which they work and live. Life has very little to offer to them: street peddling street warfare, begging or theft. Due to their misuse for illegal and immoral work, such as smuggling, prostitution, and so on, their personality development is impaired and suffer from character-disorder, a disability which cannot be seen visually. Hence, there is not much sympathy for them as is the case with, for instance, the disabled children. Out of the 27 priority areas of work in the field of children, street children have been accorded the 23rd priority. The work for helping such children requires sensitivity from the police, employers, the government and the general public, which is often lacking. All runaways working children have the basic requirement of secured spaces and a secure childhood. Neither the different organisations perceive these needs nor do our cities have the required infrastructure to cope with the needs of street and working children.

10. Summary

The organisations studied differ in their opinion regarding total elimination of child labour and this accounts for the diversity of aims and approaches to the problem. For instance, while BMM and SACCS aim at the elimination of child labour and restoring to all children the right to primary education, Butterflies, SBT, SSI are not in favour of an immediate ban on all forms of child labour since they believe that without work poor children face starvation. We would like to label the first category of NGOs as "radical" and the second category of NGOs as "protectionist", since the former group wants to alter the social structure and create one in which there is no child labour, while the latter wants to help child labourers within the existing setup by regulating their working conditions and fulfilling their basic needs of education and health care.

Advocates of the strategy of putting an outright ban on child labour system believes that such a radical action is needed when a section of the society continuous to be socially and economically exploited. They view child labour as a part of the larger system of inequality and exploitation present in the Indian society. "Radical" NGOs believe that it is not sufficient to just providing relief to the child labourers. One has to strike at the very root cause of the problem of child labour. In order to achieve this, besides releasing, rescuing and rehabilitating child labourers, these NGOs get engrossed in reforming the existing unequal structure of the society by fighting against the social problems like the caste system, the bonded labour system and alcoholism, the factors that cause and perpetuate child labour.

The "protectionist" organisations believe that the working children need support to meet their educational, nutritional, health and vocational needs. They also believe that these children need skills and information necessary to earn a living wage and fight for their rights to survive with dignity. These organisations, just like the "radical" organisations, consider child labour as bad and exploitative. However, their strategy of dealing with the problem differs significantly. Such NGOs, instead of joining together to create a revolution in the society against child labour, want to wait for the situation when child labour is totally eliminated and until then, prefer to fulfill the working children's needs of "food, security, health, love and education, a place to play and perchance to dream".

These "protectionist" NGOs have the stereotypical notion about the prevalence of child labour. Poverty is recognised as one of the main causes of child labour, since children are often required to make significant monetary or labour contributions to their families. That poverty has not deterred other countries in eliminating child labour has been shown earlier in this chapter. Besides poverty, the tradition of child labour is a strong incentive for the continuation of child labour — for both employers and parents frequently do not see anything greatly wrong in the traditional practice of child labour. Also, there are many shortcomings in the education system of our country that helps perpetuate child labour. Schools may not be available near home; curricula and teaching may be of poor quality and do not provide useful labour market skill. Given these ground realities, it is felt that any attempt at banning of child labourers, without eliminating the underlying reasons for the supply of child labour, is bound to fail as such dismissed children are likely to end up in another job. Thus, it is being increasingly recognised by most of the NGOs studied, except BMM and SACCS, that while the abolition of child labour should be an overriding objective of the public policy, sustained efforts should be carried out to provide protection and assistance to the children who are at work.

However, there is a basic similarity among the projects taken up by the NGOs, in their conception of child worker's needs and the ways of meeting them. The policies and programmes are conceived with a clear appreciation of, and certain assumptions about, the role of the child in a developing society and the many constraining factors with which the child has to cope. Almost all of the NGOs studied view the child workers as having several needs for their emotional, intellectual and physical development. The approach taken, therefore, is one, which aims at meeting the developmental needs of the child through a package of services, ranging from recreation to participation in community life.

The survey has also revealed that the NGOs are greatly dependent on institutional funding sources particularly the foreign contributions and governmental funding. This dependency leads to an atmosphere of uncertainty among the NGOs about the continuation of their projects and plans. NGOs surveyed have not been able to become self-sustainable in funding. They have tried to generate resources by way of motivating the community to sponsor their target children. But very few people come forward to sponsor a child. NGOs are not able to successfully convince and guarantee the people that their donations, if channelised through them, will be utilised properly.

The NGOs surveyed also faces the problem of proper rehabilitation of child labourers. Through their NFE programmes and their shelter homes, they try to protect and mainstream these children with the society, but they are not able to give a viable atmosphere to the children after they complete their education and training. At the same time, these NGOs integrate their NFE children with the children of the government schools, in spite of the fact that the standard of education in the latter is very poor, and that these children soon unlearn whatever they have learnt in the NFE centres of these NGOs.

The "radical" NGOs which are engaged in rescuing child labourers from the clutches of their exploitative masters do not pay similar importance to the rehabilitation of the rescued children, who, again join the labour market. This is because of the governmental apathy as well as the improper follow-up of the rescued children by these NGOs.

These "radical" NGOs are not able to achieve their goals since the general attitude of the masses is an acceptance of child labourers as a necessary evil. There is insensitivity towards the rights and needs of the working children by police, employers, government functionaries, social workers and the general public. Part of the fault lies with the NGOs themselves who have not been able to sufficiently sensitise the community against the evil of child labour system and its consequences for the concerned child labourers and the society.

Despite these limitations, what we see from the analysis of the initiatives taken by the NGOs is that all these organisations are doing their best in their own way by making use of the limited resources at their disposal. They are trying to ameliorate the conditions of working children but, with a few exceptions, are not making a dent at the underlying causes that lead to child labour. Also they are working in isolation, seldom coming together to share their strategies, experiences and achievements with others. Thus, there is a need of some sort of a co-ordination among the NGOs in order to strengthen dispersed activities and direct efforts into commonly agreed action programmes.

REFERENCES

1. Myron Weiner, *The Child and the State in India*, Oxford University Press, New Delhi, 1991.
2. Botswana, Cameroon, Equatorial Guinea, Gabon, Gambia, Ghana, Ivory Coast, Lesotho, Libya, Madagascar, Mauritius, Reunion, Rwanda, Swaziland, Zambia, and Zimbabwe have literacy rates in the 50 per cent to 75 per cent range. China, which had an illiteracy rate comparable to that of India fifty years ago, now has half the illiteracy rate of India. South Korea and Taiwan moved toward universal and compulsory education while their per capita incomes were close to that of India. (Source: Myron Weiner, *The Child and the State in India*, Oxford University Press, New Delhi, 1991).
3. Joseph Vackayil, "Indian Government Debating ILO Convention on Child Labour", *Financial Express*, July 30, 2000.
4. Neera Burra, *Born to Work: Child Labour in India*, Oxford University Press, Delhi, 1995, p. 245.
5. Based on the interviews and literature of the NGOs under study.
6. Oxfam (US) in case of Prayas.
7. For instance Friends of the DBS (UK) and Wye and Brooke India Trust (UK).
8. The sponsorship amount is specified by the concerned NGOs in their Sponsorship Forms. For instance, Deepalaya appeals for a Perpetual Sponsorship for Rs. 13,000 (India) / 16,000 (NRI), $ 560 / 400 Pounds.
9. *CRY in Action*, 3 (2), 1996.
10. Ibid.
11. *CRY in Action*, 3 (2), 1996.
12. The Ministry of Human Resource Development, Government of India, to offer academic, general and vocational programmes upto pre-degree level, established national Open School in 1989 as an autonomous institution. It is also empowered to hold its own exams and certify students who qualify for external examinations.
13. The founders of SBT were from theatre; hence boys here are encouraged to join theatres. Some boys have made their names in this field; the details are given in Chapter 6.
14. Burra, Neera, Born to Work: Child Labour in India, Oxford University Press, Delhi, 1995, p. 245.
15. NGOs such as Butterflies, Ankur and CASP do not agree with this kind of charitable teaching. They want the community, to contribute for their children's education.
16. Prayas Brochure.
17. The Helpline Service has been discussed in detail in Chapter 7.
18. CCFCL would like to take up a comparative study of China and India, investigate how child labour problem is being tackled in China and through what policies and implementation machinery. Similarly, SACCS wants to

undertake child labour studies in those industries such as sports industries in which very little work has been done till now.

19. As told by Ms. Jaya Srivastava, Director of Ankur.
20. Mobile Crèche has praised the work of Swami Agnivesh of BMM.
21. Prayas considers itself as a replicable model.
22. According to the Director of Mobile Crèches, "Definition of child labour is very politicised and blown out. We employ our beneficiary children for cleaning up of the crèche but are criticised for using child labour. This is because anything and everything is labelled as child labour".

5

Bandhua Mukti Morcha
A Case Study

Bandhua Mukti Morcha (BMM) is one of the leading NGOs of India, which campaigns for child's rights and for a complete ban on child labour. According to it: "The solution of child labour problem lies in universal elementary education, banning child labour and raising minimum wages of parents of child labourers"[1] . The organisation, though focussed on bonded and child labour is active in campaigning against multifarious social problems plaguing our country, viz. alcoholism, dowry system, low status of women, religious orthodoxy, caste war, etc. BMM has pioneered the cause of child labour and from it developed another organisation, known as the South Asian Association on Child Servitude, devoted exclusively to child labour. The informing principles of BMM are: fairness/equality in all spheres regardless of caste, creed and gender; fair and just wages to workers; rights of the child to dream; play, to go to school and emphasis on spirituality rather than on a specific religion. BMM is an example of charismatic personality-based organisation, being run on the ideas and philosophy of the founder and Chairperson, Swami Agnivesh. The organisation is also an example of how the desire to help the poor workers at a stone quarry in Faridabad led to more such missions and how it developed from a loose structure to a well-developed formal structure with 50 Staff members. BMM is engaged in rescue and release of child labourers besides rehabilitating them and hence is unique among the different NGOs that have been studied in the present work. It has its units in Uttar Pradesh, Rajasthan, Haryana, Madhya Pradesh, Karnataka, Tamil Nadu and Andhra Pradesh, which follow the same agenda and strategy. At the 7, Jantar Mantar Road, New Delhi, is situated the Secretariat of the BMM. For this study, visits were made to the Secretariat and the eight model schools at Faridabad. In Delhi itself, BMM has initiated a new project to educate the slum children of Garhi (near Nehru Place). The school was started in December 1998, the time when the authors had started the research in BMM. The authors volunteered to work for the organisation along with a South African volunteer. This was of significant bearing on the research, since insight was gained into the working of the organisation. BMM is more an action-oriented NGO – conducting raids and rescuing child labourers from factories employing child labour – the slum school is a departure from its earlier activity. However, the slum school has brought BMM at par with other child labour NGOs of Delhi, that work in the slums to prevent slum children getting involved in works at a tender age.

1. History and Progress

BMM came into being in the year 1981. The following is an account of the establishment of BMM:

> Swami Agnivesh and Prof. Sheotaj Singh (General Secretary, BMM) were in the Management Committee of 'Gurukul Indraprastha' — a residential School imparting knowledge of Vedas and Sanskrit – situated at Delhi-Haryana Border. The areas around it are mountain ranges of Aravali, where stone quarries are located. On the way to the school, both used to see the quarry workers and the pitiable conditions in which they worked. They did not have any basic amenities like safe drinking water, medical facilities, schools for children and the like. On talking to the labourers, it came to light that they have been slaves of the miners for the last 20 years. The workers were not aware of their exploitation. The only solution that Swami Agnivesh could think of was to make the labourers aware of their rights and to organise them so that unitedly they could put up a fight against the miners. Hence, Swami Agnivesh along with Prof. Sheotaj Singh started organising the workers. In the brick kilns of Haryana, Uttar Pradesh, and Rajasthan, the same slave like conditions prevailed and so they expanded their range of activities. As their work expanded they needed an office from where they could control

and supervise. And hence the organisation named Bandhua Mukti Morcha or Bonded Labour Liberation Front came into being.

BMM was initially housed in Haryana Bhawan from 1977-82. This was the period when Swami Agnivesh was Janata Party MLA in the Haryana Legislative Assembly and being a Swami he never had a home or any property of his own. Hence, he was living in the Haryana Bhawan and operating the organisation from there. Then for a brief period the office was shifted to the South Avenue. However, since 1981, it is located at 7, Jantar Mantar Road, New Delhi. It got registered as a Society under the Societies Registration Act 1860 in 1994. By working towards organising the bonded labourers, Swami Agnivesh and Prof. Singh realised that there was no legislation for quarry workers. This pushed them to fight a case in the Supreme Court (Bandhua Mukti Morcha versus Union of India and others). In 1982, the Supreme Court gave a landmark judgement giving the Centre and the State Governments twenty-one directions, ordering them to rescue and rehabilitate the bonded quarry workers. It also constituted various committees to inquire about the conditions of such workers. However, BMM is still battling the case for the provision of basic facilities to the quarry workers. It has opened up schools for children of such workers since in its absence children are also engaged in mining.

On asking Swami Agnivesh about how and when child labourers were included in BMM's agenda, Swamiji said that in 1983 they rescued 32 bonded child labourers between the ages of six and fourteen from carpet manufacturers of Mirzapur District, Uttar Pradesh. BMM organised a National Convention in the Village 'Paneri Bandh', District Palamu, Bihar. Near the village was situated the 'Chichchori' village in which these rescued bonded child labourers resided who used to work for 18 hours a day in the carpet industry. They had been tortured for making mistakes, hung upside down and branded with red hot rods. These children were invited at the Convention where they told their tale in front of eminent personalities like Mahashweta Devi, delegates from ILO, Trade Union leaders and newspaper journalists. As a result, this case got wide publicity and was debated in both the Indian Parliament and the United Nations Commission on Human Rights. BMM filed a Petition (No. 121125) in 1984, in the Supreme Court. The Supreme Court ordered the district administration to secure the release of these children 32 children. It also appointed Prem Bhai (prominent social worker in Mirzapur, Uttar Pradesh), to investigate the conditions of child labourers in scattered small villages. The Prem Bhai Commission's finding revealed that there were 75,000 child labourers in the carpet belt in Uttar Pradesh. The Commissions' report corroborated the BMM submissions and exposed the non-implementation of protective legislation. Thus, from this chance discovery of child labourers, BMM included the issue of child labour in its agenda. According to Swami Agnivesh, "any child not going to school, working for six or more hours and not getting minimum wages, is a bonded child labour".

BMM has raised voice for 50 lakh bonded and stone quarry workers. For BMM, bonded workers means not only those who are owned and whose services are controlled by another person, but also all those workers who do not get minimum wages and who work for more than eight hours. Hence, all child workers for BMM are also bonded workers. Accordingly, BMM has calculated that there are 65 million child labourers in the carpet industry, bangle making, match industry, diamond industry, brass and steel polishing in garages, *dhaba*s, as domestic servants and other urban sector works who work for more than eight hours with no fixed wages. For the rights of such children BMM has been constantly raising awareness at the public level as well as at the government level.

BMM, through direct action, raids and legal recourse, has been able to rescue more than 7000 children from Mirzapur-Bhadohi carpet belt. BMM has also mounted consumers' awareness campaign in Europe and the United States, the main markets for carpets. The consumers demand for a label on each carpet guaranteeing 'free of child labour', created tremendous pressure on both the foreign importers, domestic exporters/manufactures. It also roused the conscience of planners, politicians and humanists, of the developed countries.

BMM, along with other NGOs, and in collaboration with Indo-German Export Promotion (IGEP) sponsored an initiative for setting up a Rugmark Foundation entrusted with the responsibility of inspection, monitoring and labelling of carpets so as to seek exemption from the provision of legislation of the importing country banning import of products made by children.

Hence, we see, BMM has been fighting against the scourge of bonded and child labour for the past 19 years.

2. The Founder

BMM was founded in 1981 by Swami Agnivesh, who has been (as a reporter puts it), "the Don Quixote of the movements against bonded labour, sati, ban on entry of Dalits into temples and consumption of liquor. Relentlessly striving for an *Arya Rashtra* (physical, spiritual and social well being of the entire world), debunking religious orthodoxy and wanting culture to be the instrument to fight injustice and poverty".[2]

Swami Agnivesh was born into an orthodox Telugu-speaking family on September 21, 1939. He earned a Master's Degree in Commerce and a Law Degree from Calcutta. After a brief stint as a Professor of Business Management and Company Law at St. Xavier's College, Calcutta, he was inspired to join the Arya Samaj Movement. The activities of the Samaj influenced his life and finally in 1969, donning the robes of a '*sadhu*' (monk), he left for Haryana. It was at this time that he changed his original name Vepa Shyam Rao to Swami Agnivesh.[3]

Within a couple of hours of attaining *Sanyas*, Swami Agnivesh along with Swami Indravesh, founded a Political Party called the Arya Sabha, a unit of the Arya Samaj to fight religious dogmatism and social evil through politics.[4] The Party in a year became a recognised regional party. Swami Agnivesh did not see any contradiction in being a religious missionary and a political activist at the same time and has codified his views under the name of "*vedic socialism*".[5] He summed up his beliefs as follows:

> "Arya Samaj does not believe in a ritualistic and dogmatic view of religion but has stood for values like truth, non-violence, non-accumulation. So unless and until there is a fundamental change in the socio-economic system, our religious ideals are impossible to achieve. Therefore, our pursuit is closely linked to the pursuit for social change; our concept of non-violence imbibed in us a spirit of struggle against forces of violence including socio-economic exploitation. I want to inculcate in the people the spirit of doubt, debate and dissent".

His party, Arya Sabha was in the forefront of many struggles in Haryana and in 1974 Jaya Prakash Narayan spotted them and asked them to lead the Haryana Chapter of the Samagraha Kranti Morcha. He was jailed during the emergency and in jail was deeply influenced by the writings of Mahatma Gandhi. Swami Agnivesh was particularly impressed by Gandhi's "*Antyodaya*" concept, which said one should begin with the last man, the poorest of the poor.

In 1977, on the advice of Jaya Prakash Narayan, Arya Sabha merged with the Janata Party and Swami Agnivesh won the Pundari seat in Haryana's Kurukshetra District on a Janata ticket. He was even made the Education Minister of Haryana in 1979. However, he resigned within three months, protesting against police firing on workers in Faridabad. His act won him many enemies within the party and he was expelled after a few years.

The attitude of Swami Agnivesh to remain alive to the problems of the people, led to the setting up of Bandhua Mukti Morcha in 1981. Swami Agnivesh says:

> "I believe that spiritual and social values have to be 'rekindled' in the masses. And we have to start from the lowest of levels. That is why we took up the task of liberating quarry and brick kiln workers. They are not properly organised and are being exploited to the maximum extent possible".

At the quarry and brick kilns in Faridabad, women and children were mostly engaged in carrying stones from the mines. Parents were dissuaded by the employers from sending their children to school, and instead were forced to earn their daily bread. Hence, Swami Agnivesh opened up schools for the children of quarry and brick kiln workers. And thus, started his struggle against bonded and child labour along with the basic issues which gave rise to this evil.

3. Influence of Arya Samaj on BMM

Swami Agnivesh's life sketch, described above, shows a deep impact of Arya Samaj Movement over him. The spirit of social and religious reform that the Arya Samaj founder, Swami Dayanand Saraswati, expounded inspired Swami Agnivesh so much so that he decided to focus on this aspect even after joining the religious order and taking the necessary vows. Hence, the activities of his organisation — BMM – have been influenced by the philosophy of Arya Samaj. "Arya Samaj does not believe in a ritualistic and dogmatic view of religion but has stood for values like truth, non-violence, non-accumulation. So unless and until there is a fundamental change in the socio-economic system, our religious ideals are impossible to achieve. Therefore, our pursuit of religion was closely linked to the pursuit for social change, our concept of non-violence imbibed in us a spirit of struggle against forces of violence including socio-economic exploitation".[6]

Hence, he and his organisation is engaged in not only elimination of child labour, bonded labour, poverty but also mobilises people to protest against corruption in high places, dowry system, bride burning, the increasing influence of westernised lifestyles, casteism, religious fundamentalism and alcoholism. Swami Agnivesh does not view these issues in isolation but links them to social, economic and political issues and trends. For instance, according to him, the problem of child labour is closely related to bonded labour, which in turn is related to the caste system. As he puts it:

> "Almost all victims of child labour are children of the parents who were bonded labour, though they may not be legally identified. The Joint Survey of the Gandhi Peace Foundation and the National Labour Institute established for the first time in 1979 that 86 per cent of bonded labour belongs either to the Scheduled Castes or the Scheduled Tribes. So the pernicious caste system is very much responsible for the perpetuation of bonded and child labour system. One of the main reasons of why our ruling elite took twenty five years to enact a legislation against the bonded labour system and why after 25 years of this deterrent Act, not much progress could be made by way of abolishing bonded labour system is because the ruling elite, consisting of the Brahmins, the Kshatriyas and the Vaishyas, consider the Shudras expandable. This appalling mindset is responsible for the callousness of bureaucracy towards social change and therefore, a fight against the abominable caste system becomes integral to the fight against child labour system.
>
> Similarly, the fight for gender justice and the fight against alcoholism, fundamentalism, westernised lifestyles, reinforce BMM's commitment to fight against child labour. Alcoholism is largely responsible for dropout of children from schools who then

go for earning. The root of all of our problems is the paradigm of our development, which is becoming more and more materialistic and less and less spiritual. This lopsided materialistic development and the resultant destruction of the ecology are also causing land alienation, large-scale migration of labour and impoverishment of rural poor. The big dams and such other mega projects have displaced millions of rural poor without any proper rehabilitation. These poor, end up as landless agricultural labourers, migrant labourers, contract labourers and bonded labourers and their children become victims of child bonded labour. Thus, all these issues are interrelated."

However, the association of Arya Samaj with BMM is only at the philosophical level. No person in the organisation is forced to become an Arya Samaji, although the General Secretary and some of the field workers are Arya Samajis. But not all of them are monks. Also, there is no subtle discrimination favouring Arya Samajis in the organisation. Swami Agnivesh understands that social work may be done devotionally only when one is free of familial responsibilities and wants his workers to be so. But this is not forced. For instance, a school teacher at BMM's School at Garhi (Delhi), working since December 1998, has been so much influenced by Swami Agnivesh that recently (August 1999), he has decided to remain a celibate and to keep serving children throughout his life.

4. Philosophy and Objectives of BMM

The mission of BMM is to mobilise people to raise their voice for their rights. BMM does not believe in charity for the poor, but in making them self-sufficient. BMM's aims and objectives[7] are as follows:

1. Identification, release and rehabilitation of bonded labour in various sectors of the economy.
2. To form unions of labourers in various sectors of economy.
3. To educate people against repression, injustice and atrocities through peaceful awareness building.
4. To acquaint people about the prohibitive laws banning bonded system.

5. To promote feelings of brotherhood, unity and build public opinion against religious bigotry and communal frenzy.
6. To protect rights of citizens and to generate awareness against political exploitation and corruption.
7. To build lobby against child marriage, child labour, dowry, caste system and other social evils.
8. To propagate Indian culture, art languages and to advocate for adequate livelihood.
9. To work for communal unity and integrity.
10. To promote cooperation and solidarity among social organisations engaged in social justice and to struggle for seeking social and economic justice for all.

On the issue of child labour, BMM's philosophy is very clear. It calls for a total ban on child labour system for the proper growth and development of children and the society, in general. The General Secretary gave the following account of the cause of child servitude thus exploding the myth of poverty leading to child labour thesis. The argument he presented is as follows. "Child servitude arises owing to socio-economic and historical reasons. It is believed that four factors, viz. poverty, unemployment, over-population and illiteracy are the main reasons for this pernicious system. But our experience and the various studies conducted by researchers corroborate the fact that child servitude is equally if not solely responsible for causing and perpetuating unemployment, poverty, population growth and illiteracy. There is a correlation between child labour and unemployed adults since Independence. In 1947 the number of child labourers was approximately 10 million and the unemployed adults also were of the same magnitude. Now, child labour has touched the 60 million mark, and the figure of unemployed adults has also soared to the same level. Therefore, if we do not eradicate the child servitude today, we would be responsible for perpetuating poverty, abject misery and sickness of 65 million adults in the country".[8] This derivation of the cause and effect of child labour forms BMM's philosophy and mission to combat child labour.

BMM has been pressing the government to abolish the distinction between hazardous and non-hazardous forms of child labour. The Child Labour Protection and Regulation Act of 1986 covers only children working in intolerable conditions and not other child labour. As such, any attempts by NGOs to end child labour in any form as mandated in the constitution and prohibitive laws have proved futile because of many escape routes in the relevant laws. BMM has been opposing such a line of approach. Children working for 10 to 16 hours a day too come under the category of hazardous in real sense as long working hours adversely affect their health, mental, physical and moral development, thereby reducing their span of life. In the long run, these factors out weigh the short gains acquired by employment of children.

Hence, BMM calls for a total ban on child labour since by banning it, an equivalent number of unemployed adults (65 million as estimated by BMM in 1998) would get employment who in turn, can demand more money and better working conditions. This would lead to improvement in their living condition and they would send their children to the schools.

BMM's philosophy regarding the best strategy to deal with the issue of child labour is to provide meaningful education to all children. The Policy Statement of BMM talks about combating child labour through food for education and states the following points:

1. Children who are being denied their fundamental right to education and are labouring for eight or more hours a day are bonded child labourers and need deliverance on priority basis under Article 32 of UN Convention on the Rights of the Child and Article 45 of the Indian Constitution.
2. We call for the immediate provision of Fundamental Rights to Education. We urge the Government to commit themselves to free and compulsory elementary education for all children upto the age of fourteen (with training in productive skills). This is a Constitutional Mandate enshrined in Article 24, 39 (e), (f) and 45. Article 45 is very specific about the Government's responsibility to provide education to all children between the age of 6 and 14 within a period of 10 years, i.e. by 1960.
3. Successive Governments since 1950 have been found criminally callous and negligent in carrying out this mandate, thereby, accentuating the problem of child servitude.

4. Any pretence of non-formal education for two hours or so has the danger of only legitimising the child labour system. We should, instead, integrate the skills a child is learning as part of family labour or otherwise, along side his or her full time schooling into the formal education system. For effective implementation, a task force of committed NGOs should be constituted in all the States.
5. In order to attract all the child labourers to such schools (as mentioned in point no. 4) and to guard against drop-outs, a 'Food for Education Scheme' should be launched with at least one kilogram of rice or wheat to every child for every day of schooling. (This would also take care of the essential food security, obviating hunger in the disadvantaged communities and provide the necessary "staying power" to the parents for organising themselves against the scourge/vagaries of bonded labour system). The ultimate answers to most of our problems lie in organising the unorganised, mobilising them for social justice and gender equity. The voiceless millions should be able to raise their voice loud and clear.

5. Organisational Structure

Established in 1981, BMM has expanded its activities in eight States, Delhi being the Head Office or the Secretariat. These State Units are in Karnataka, Andhra Pradesh, Maharashtra, Rajasthan, Haryana, Madhya Pradesh, Uttar Pradesh and Bihar. There is a constant interaction among them and the Secretariat and its workers are often called to attend seminars, meetings, programmes, and such other events. In the yearly "*Chaupal*" (meeting), the strategy of work is intimated to the State Units, which are to function accordingly.

Initially, BMM was a loosly knit organisation. Although its workers are spread all over the country, its regular workers are 50. The Management comprises of a President/Chairperson, Vice President, General Secretary, Treasurer and 15 Members.

The structure of the Delhi Secretariat is as follows:

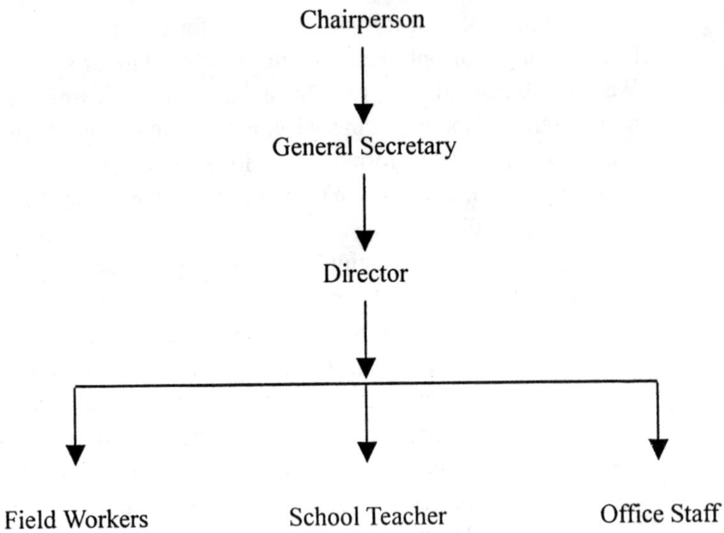

The Secretariat office staff included: a computer operator, an accountant, a receptionist, a person for documenting newspaper articles on BMM and its activities, a peon and a cook.

The Chairperson as also the President, Swami Agnivesh is in overall in charge of the organisation and it is his philosophy and ideas that runs the organisation. He decides the broad policy of the organization and prescribes the focus areas and parameters of the programmes that the staff develops and pursues. The General Secretary, Prof. Sheotaj Singh, who is an Arya Samaji, is associated with the organisation since its inception. He supervises schools for children freed from labour or children of former bonded labourers. He also devises new projects, organises seminars, rallies, conferences with the help of his staff. He also deals with correspondences regarding the projects, schools, seminars and the issue of invitations to several events organised by the BMM. The Director is a retired Government Officer, who supervises teachers and field workers, oversees the use of funds for projects and deals with correspondence related to projects. The field workers or social workers at the different State units are engaged in rescue, release and rehabilitation of child and bonded labourers, and decisions on all such activities are taken at the Secretariat. The state units have to send their work reports every month.

But in actuality, the Director keeps reminding them to send their reports by writing letters to them. Except the Karnataka unit, which can generate its own finances, all the other units are financially dependent on the Secretariat.

5.1 Recruitment

For its field staff, BMM does not have any formal procedure of recruitment and those who are interested in action-oriented work of BMM, approach it, according to the General Secretary. The past records and work experiences of the interested candidates are analysed and according to their area of interest, tasks are allotted. For its field activities, BMM needs people who can organise the unorganised, listen to their problems, and get bonded workers and child labourers released and rescued. For such work, no formal education is required. Hence, as the General Secretary puts it: "The social workers could be illiterate or be degree holders in social work". However, there is no staff of the latter category, which may be due to the low pay scale of the organisation. Also the term of employment for field staff is temporary, they are kept on probation for some months before retaining them in service.

For the technical staff, there is a formal process of recruitment. The technical staff in the organisation includes the accountant, typists and computer-operators. Such posts are advertised in leading newspapers and interviews conducted, but the final decision is made by the Chairperson.

5.2 Staff Turnover

The General Secretary complained about the lack of committed workers. According to him, "a project, which we undertake needs to give some outcome so that we can be answerable to the funding agencies, but if the staff leave, the project suffers." He holds that corrupt NGOs can afford to pay their staff lavishly to ensure that they do not complain of corruption at the top. He says that his workers are also attracted to the high paying but corrupt NGOs, and hence it is difficult to get committed workers. He also boasts that in its history of 17 years, no BMM member has been asked to leave. People have quit voluntarily on getting government jobs or jobs in other NGOs. He strongly believes that the money given by funding agency should be utilised for the target group and not for staff and the lavish maintenance of office. While it is possible to find replacement for those who leave the job, the low remuneration offered to the staff adversely affects their commitment to the organisation.

5.3 Rule Adherence

The organisation has a written Constitution having bye-laws and rules regarding how to conduct elections, the violation of which may lead to the de-registration of the organisation.

At the Secretariat, each member of the staff has his or her own sphere of work. The Director does the overall supervision. Swami Agnivesh and the General Secretary coordinate all the tasks and attend programmes and meetings plus visit the State units.

The field worker, who oversees the BMM's work in Faridabad stone quarries, does not follow any fixed schedule. He might be called to the Secretariat, at any time of the day or the night, by the Chairperson or the quarry workers or the union leaders in Faridabad.

5.4 Hierarchy,Bureaucracy and Decision-making

The General Secretary's response to hierarchy in the organisation was that because the organisation is headed by a '*sanyasi*' (monk), there is no hierarchy and that the workers are not treated as employees but as co-workers/associates. Among the staff, there is no hierarchy and all are at the same plane. But at the top level, there exists a hierarchy, with the highest authority being vested in Swami Agnivesh. The authors noticed that while addressing the staff, their names were suffixed with '*ji*', the Hindi word for respect.

BMM is a personality-based organisation and it is the charisma of Swami Agnivesh that attracts the funding agencies. It is his ideology that rules the organisation. He is the sole authority in decision-making.

However, the field/social workers at the State units are free to take decisions concerning certain trivial issues. For instance, the field worker in charge of the Faridabad schools and of the worker's union told me that he is free to take decisions on local matters such as repairing the water tap, helping children in being enrolled at schools and the like. But he has to inform/report to Swami Agnivesh on the work he does. However, in getting the help of District Collectors or other Labour Officers, Swami Agnivesh's help and guidance is sought. Similarly, the school teachers are free to take decisions regarding how to teach but for issues pertaining to finances e.g. buying of notebooks, slates, pencils, etc., they are dependent upon the Secretariat and it takes some time before the items are procured.

Sometimes there are clashes in decision making between the Chairperson and the General Secretary. For instance, once the South African volunteer and the authors were to go to the slum children's School at Garhi. Since it was their first visit, they did not know the way to the school and so, the Accountant of BMM had agreed to come with us. Swami Agnivesh had given the permission to the Accountant to accompany us. But when they were about to leave, the General Secretary tried to prevent the Accountant from coming with us by instructing him to complete his work. It was at that time that Swami Agnivesh intervened and told the General Secretary that as he had already checked up with the Accountant that there was no urgent work pending, he could be sent to guide the volunteers to the Garhi School.

5.5 Internal Conflict

We were told that there was no internal conflict in the organisation and if any conflict arises among members of the Staff, it is resolved by talking to the concerned parties. However, the personal ambition of one of its prominent members, led to a split in the BMM, with the member setting up of his own organisation.

This member was the former General Secretary (G.S.) of BMM and Swami Agnivesh has great faith in him. The G.S. was on field most of the time claiming to be releasing and rescuing child labourers. However, a journalist exposed his misadventure. The Sunday Observer in its January issue[9], summed up the story as follows:

> "In September, Mr. abc[10], a prominent member of the organisation was gheroed by the Fourth Estate for parading a 'fraud' orphan

claimed to have freed. A prominent South Indian daily played up the story, which led to the child being granted a donation from the Prime Minister's Relief Fund. A few days later a regional correspondent of the particular newspaper discovered that the child was no orphan or bonded labour".

This revelation led Swami Agnivesh to expel him from the organisation.

5.6 Networking

BMM networks with the like-minded organisations, viz., Butterflies, Participatory Research in Asia, Narmada Bachao Andolan and Arya Samaj. These organisations are invited for its meetings and programmes and in turn, the representatives of BMM, attends programmes organised by these institutions.

5.7 Project Selection

The most recent of BMM's project is a vocational cum residential centre in Faridabad for the former child labourers, between the age-group of 12-14 years. They are to be trained in different crafts and trades such as welding, plumbing, motor mechanics and in-house wiring. Along with it, non-formal education is also to be provided to teach the children basic literacy. These projects were inspired by similar ones, initiated in other countries. The project is located near Gurukul Indraprastha (Faridabad). It is the same place at which Swami Agnivesh and the General Secretary had settled the labourers who had been released from bondage from the nearby stone quarries. The finances for this project were mobilised through Swami Agnivesh's personal contacts. This kind of work does not antagonise the government/state. At the same time, this kind of institutional care provides visibility to the work done. Hence, people are willing to donate to such projects. For instance, the German Stern TV Channel, which produces Documentaries on children's issues and appeals to the general public to help children in distress, generously provided financial assistance for this project.

6. Activities of BMM

6.1 Early Activities

In the initial period, the founders were involved in organising and fighting for the bonded workers of stone quarries and brick kilns in Faridabad, Uttar Pradesh. They organised meeting for these workers. Initially the employers used to frighten them and threatened of turning them out of work, but gradually workers realised that their condition could not get worse than what was it currently. The employers could at best turn them out but that would be beneficial for the workers, as they would then be free. The workers realised that employers need them as much as they wanted the employers. So they started coming to the meetings, organised by the founders of BMM, in which they were told about their rights and how to demand it. The awareness building led workers to come together and form a union to defend their rights. At present the stone quarry and construction workers are united into two unions, respectively the *Rashtriya Khan Mazdoor* Union and the Construction Workers Union.

According to the founders, the support from the Press and subsequently the highest Judiciary brought about the initial success in their endeavour. But the attitude of the then Chief Minister of Haryana, Mr. Bhajan Lal and the bureaucracy at the level of District Magistrate who has the powers under bonded labour Act, was very unhelpful. On asking to introspect on the strategies that were a failure and that succeeded, Swami Agnivesh's response was:

> "The strategy of legal redressal to which we relied too much on, proved not to be so effective particularly, when we know that India has 65 million child labourers. Under the Bonded Labour System Abolition Act of 1976, the legal procedure is identification, release and rehabilitation of bonded child labour, followed up by prosecution of employer, but it cannot be used in every case. Therefore, we have realised that providing good, relevant and quality education to every child upto 14 years, is a better and more effective way of eliminating child labour".

6.2 Current Activities and initiatives

The activities of BMM as stated in its Brochure are as follows:

6.2.1 *Release and Rehabilitation*

BMM claims to have been successful in releasing nearly 1,24,000 bonded labourers. A large number of them have been rehabilitated. It has rescued about a thousand children, most of them migrants from the carpet industry.

Here a brief note on how the raids are conducted is necessary. There are three different stages involved in the release of bonded labourers, viz., identification, raid/rescue and rehabilitation. Information regarding bonded and child labourers is got either from the BMM activists/workers in the field or from the parents themselves. On getting the information, District Administration is made aware of it and the concerned staff of BMM, along with the police, goes to the particular place and conduct raiding operation. However, they face difficulties in the sense that the employers hide the children. Sometimes even the administration also helps employers in telling them in advance of the raids. So, the children are told not to reveal their true identities in front of the visiting government officials, but are asked by their employers to say that they are employer's own children. In this way the employers go scot-free, which is possible because the Child Labour (Prohibition and Regulation) Act, 1986, exempts child labour in the family enterprises. Thus, the Act permits employment of children in hazardous process if a process is undertaken by any of their family members.

The whole process of dealing with the released bonded labourers involves: meeting the labourers, talking to them and also educating them about their rights, minimum wages, etc., taking a written statement from each one about their conditions of employment; and simultaneously informing the District Magistrate and the District Collector and providing with detailed evidence on their arrival, thus mobilising the local administration to issue release certificates to the rescued workers. As specified in the relevant Acts, in the absence of a release certificate a rescued bonded labour cannot get ex-gratia and transit camp facilities till the time he is transported back to his native place. Further, he is also not eligible for rehabilitation benefits. The process also involves inviting the journalists from the press and the prominent TV channels to cover the interviews of the rescued workers and finally, follow-up of the entire case until there is some result, i.e., till the workers are rehabilitated and action is taken against their employers.

Such activities may also be clarified by the following illustration of the raid and rescue operations conducted by the Ferozabad unit and the Bhiwani (Haryana) unit of BMM.[11]

Ferozabad is a mega-production center for glass and bangle articles with heavy concentration of child labour. In April 1998, the Ferozabad unit of BMM conducted a surprise visit to one of the glass factories there. It was found that this factory had 50 child workers besides adult workers. It was learned subsequently that the owner of the factory dispensed with the services of adult labourers. The unit intervened in the matter and got released those 50 children from the clutches of the owner but they were not issued any release certificates by the local administration.

In another case, the Bhiwani unit of BMM organised a raid at the stone quarries Charkhi Dadri, Dist. Bhiwani, Haryana on the 26th July 1997 and rescued 160 bonded labourers including men, women and children. The belt of stone quarries especially Bhiwani abounds in bonded workers. As narrated by the rescued workers, they had been working in these quarries for the last 2 to 15 years. They were members of the Scheduled Tribes from Guna (Madhya Pradesh). A few families hailed from Jhansi (Uttar Pradesh) and Kota (Rajasthan). These bonded labourers were promised Rs. 240/- per truck load including stones breaking, loading etc. But they were not paid any wages. They were provided only the ration of *atta* (wheat flour) and *dal* (pulses) through agents. The employers' musclemen kept a watch on them and they were quiet often threatened of dire consequences if they moved out. Ironically, the local administration did not issue release certificates on demand by BMM as such a measure would have gone against the affidavit filed by the State in the Supreme Court stating that there was no bonded labour in the State. The local administration simply made them to board a train bound for Riwari. Thereafter the workers took another train and came to Sarai Rohilla, Delhi. BMM brought them over to Jantar Mantar where a tent was set up for their stay. These bonded labourers met press persons and the Secretary, Ministry of Labour to whom they explained their plight. With the intervention of the Secretary, the representative of the Government of Madhya Pradesh took steps for the dispatch of these bonded labourers to the Guna district for rehabilitation. A few of them, who belonged to Rajasthan were also sent back to their native places. BMM is still fighting a case with the respective State governments for giving the release certificate to these workers.

6.2.2 *Programmes for Child Labourers*

(a) *Schools*: BMM wants child labourers to be put into the schools and mainstreamed into the society and the development process. It is running 'Model Schools' for the children withdrawn from the industries like bangle-making, carpet weaving as well as from agriculture and stone quarries. These schools are in Gwalior, Faridabad, Maharashtra, Firozabad and Alwar.

(b) *NFE with Provision of Cereals*: BMM has also started a campaign for the provision of non-formal full time education for child workers, along with the supply of 1 kilogram of cereals to each child for each day of school. It is both an incentive and a measure of food security to their poor families. This scheme was approved by the Ministry of Labour, for the schools sponsored by it for ex-child labourers in certain industrial areas.

(c) *Vocational Training*: BMM has embarked on the programme of providing children in the age-group of 13-14 years, technical training in different trades and crafts to make them self-reliant since it believes that once children are technically qualified, no body can exploit them and they can demand better wages.

(d) *Lobbying in Parliamentary Forums*: As a result of BMM's persistent efforts, for the first time the leaders of the leading political parties showed their concern on the issue of child labour and made a mention of it in their election manifestoes in the Parliamentary Elections of 1996. The Common Minimum Programme (CMP) of the United Front Government committed itself for total elimination of all forms of child labour and to make education upto 14 years of age free and compulsory.

(e) *Awareness Generation*: BMM is engaged in the awareness generation on child labour through marches, demonstration, wall writings and holding seminars.

For instance, in Maharashtra, notorious for the preponderance of child labour, BMM conducted an awareness march to senistise people against this menace. The march was conducted in District Latur and stretched from 14th November 1998 to 20th November 1998. This march covered about a distance of 1000 kms. Every day a public meeting was held at an important place. In the march, the issue of bonded and child labour and the relevant prohibitive laws were highlighted. Besides, en-route posters, leaflets and stickers were distributed. This march created a good impact on the people.

BMM conducted a South Asian Seminar on child labour, between November 30 to December 1, 1996, in the Parliament House. The participant countries included Pakistan, Sri Lanka, and Bangladesh, besides India. South Asia has the dubious distinction of having the world's largest child labour force. The same region is also seething with unemployment, poverty, illiteracy and population explosion. What makes matters worse for them is the surreptitious role of international financial giants like the International Monetary Fund, the World Bank and the World Trade Organisation (WTO). These countries feel the introduction of 'social clause' in WTO as a further blow to their economies. The 'social clause' entails the banning and boycotting of all exportable goods and services, which involve any direct or indirect use of forced labour or child labour. The developing countries view the social clause as a veritable 'human face' of protectionism and a euphemism for a non-tariff barrier in international trade.

The South Asia Seminar on Child Labour was a landmark in the quest for solidarity among the NGOs of South Asia on the issue of child labour. According to the Chairperson, BMM, the seminar succeeded in forging new avenues for meaningful dialogue with International organisations like the ILO, UNICEF and the like. The participant countries condemned the political mechanisation operated through WTO, thereby undermining existing forums e.g., the United Nation, the Non-aligned Movement and so on. They called upon their governments to respect the mandate given to them by the people and not become slaves of the globalisation system. Further, they expressed solidarity with the struggles against privatisation/globalisation, specifically the struggles of bonded child labour and child labour. The participant countries committed to the goal of the total elimination of child labour prevalent now and prevention of more children getting involved in labour. They agreed to a Plan of Action, which targets children upto 14 years of age. Being aware that NGOs, activists and other such groups cannot on their own eliminate child labour, the modality to be pursued is to mobilize public opinion to bring about pressure on the respective National Governments to pursue policies, programmes and legislations that would lead to the prevention and elimination of child labour.

BMM also held a Seminar in August 1998 in Bhopal, Madhya Pradesh, to sensitise people, politicians and the bureaucrats of the magnitude of the problem.

(f) *Campaign for National Minimum Wage*: To mitigate the severity of the abominable system of child labour, BMM, of late, has been campaigning for a National Minimum Wage equivalent to first day salary of a new entrant class IV employee in Government service. Its revision is to be done on the cost-price-index (CPI) as is done for the Government employees. The State Governments may fix minimum wage according to the local conditions but not below National Minimum Wage.

The authors attended one such meeting at the Mavalankar Hall, New Delhi, to campaign for the minimum wages among the unorganised workers, who were called from Punjab and Haryana. The workers belonged to the Punjab Khet Mazdoor Union (agricultural worker's union) and Patthar Khadan Mazdoor Union (stone quarry worker's union, Haryana) and were brought to Delhi, by trucks, arranged by the BMM. The programme was to start at 10 a.m., but the trucks did not arrive till 11 a.m., since they were stopped at the Delhi Borders. The higher authorities were then informed about the programme and were requested an uninterrupted arrival of the trucks. The guest invitees to the programme included the Union Labour Minister Satyanarayan Jathia, trade union leaders Gurudas Dasgupta and P.K. Ganguly, Members of Parliament Ramanand Singh and Geeta Mukherjee. The workers stated their grievances and problems to the eminent guests. These included non-availability of basic necessities like water and electricity supply, ration shops, primary schools. They, especially the Punjab workers, requested the government to write off their loans since they are not in a position to pay up. The BMM members invited labourers to take out a march to Parliament to "make the government listen to their needs and demands". Chairperson Swami Agnivesh demanded that the national minimum wage for 32 crore workers in the unorganised sector be increased and be made equivalent to the first day salary of a class IV government employee. He also demanded that the government should guarantee to the workers the 'right to work' for at least 240 days in a year. The eminent invitees were favourable to these demands. The labour minister promised setting up of the 2nd Labour Commission, which would look into the problems of the unorganised workers. The workers seemed happy with the promise and went back after having lunch arranged for them by the BMM

(g) *Child Rights International*: Child rights activists and friends of BMM in the United States of America have formed a new organisation under the above name. The Department of State, State of New York, under Section 402 of the non-profit Corporation Law, on November 27, 1996 has duly registered the same. It will soon be granted "Charity Status". Child Rights International has been formed for the purpose of increasing awareness of the problem of child labour and to provide a forum for sharing ideas and generating approaches to alleviate this problem throughout the world. It will inform the media, opinion makers, elected officials, non-governmental organisations and other leaders about related issues and will serve as a network for domestic and trans-national organisations.

6.3 Monitoring of Projects

According to the General Secretary, "the field activists keep an eye on the project". Occasionally, the Chairperson or the General Secretary or a staff member may personally visit the project site. At the same time, the local people, with sympathies for the cause of the BMM, are asked to check on the work and to report if there are any complaints.

Inspite of these checks and balances, there are hindrances to the effective monitoring of the schools in Faridabad where we did our study. The schools are spread over the hilly regions of Sohna, and there are no effective transport facilities. Besides the lack of access, there is no staff with the exclusive responsibility of looking after the schools. The person, who organises the unorganised workers of stone quarry workers in Faridabad, also looks after the needs of the school. During our visit, in Pali School No. 2, the teacher complained that when he was on leave for 15 days, the previous month, there was nobody to substitute him. It was later discovered that another person had drawn 15 days salary and had utilised the biscuits sent for children for personal consumption, but had not taught the school children!

7. Finances

The following account on the financial aspects of BMM is based on information provided by its General Secretary and the Accountant.

BMM mobilises funds through individual donations. It is also implementing projects of CAPART and ILO-IPEC (International Programme on Elimination of Child Labour). CAPART is funding a project on awareness generation about bonded labour. This is under the Ministry of Labour. BMM is running 8 Schools for children of stone quarry and brick kiln workers from the funds it receives from ILO-IPEC. ILO is also funding awareness generation projects in Maharashtra, Karnataka and Uttar Pradesh. Action Aid is funding the project on Survey of Child Labour and Bonded Labour and Awareness Generation Project in Sonbhadra, Almora, Shikohabad in Uttar Pradesh. The Ministry of Labour was providing funds for women's skill development programme but it has now been discontinued because of non-availability of teachers and fewer number of women interested in cloth cutting and tailoring. Action Aid is also funding projects with the objectives such as the elimination of child labour, for fighting the evils of the dowry system, for the provision of minimum wages, and for equal rights for women, in three regions of Uttar Pradesh, viz., the carpet-making belt of Mirzapur-Bhadohi, Glass Bangle industry in Ferozabad and in the Uttarakhand region. BMM's two Schools in Sonbhadra (Uttar Pradesh) for former child labourers of the carpet industry are being run by funds from the Carpet Export Promotion Council (CEPC).

BMM also receives donations ranging from Rs. 10 to Rs. 1000 from India and abroad, owing mainly to Swami Agnivesh's charisma.

BMM often finds it difficult to sustain projects if there is delay in the release of funds by the donors. For instance, as the General Secretary quipped, BMM had to sustain the ILO-IPEC Projects through donations after the first three years, when it stopped funding. He agreed that there are strings attached to funds and said that BMM does not accept donations made with certain preconditions. The BMM, he says, does not accept funds if the funding agency wants information about the employers. BMM, however, readily furnishes information to its donors about the number of children released from bondage, number rehabilitated and educated and the details of its accounts. BMM wants to have its own corpus fund so that it becomes self-reliant. This goal is yet to be achieved and the BMM continues its 'hand to mouth existence'.

8. BMM and the State

The General Secretary of BMM agreed that those who take money from the State (or even the foreign agencies) have to work under pressure. The kind of work that BMM undertakes viz. rescue and release of child labourers, demonstrations and marches, it is in constant conflict with the State, which has vested interest in prevalence of child labour. BMM has been fighting a legal battle with the Government of Haryana over the non-provision of rehabilitation measures by the latter for the 160 bonded labourers (including 65 children), belonging to the Guna District of Madhya Pradesh, released by BMM. This case is referred to as the People's Union for Civil Liberties (PUCL) versus Union of India.

The story goes like this. The District Magistrates of 13 States (including Haryana), had issued affidavit in 1995 declaring that in their respective States, there was no bonded labour. Several NGOs in these States, however, had approached the BMM providing information about the prevalence of bonded labourers in their States. The BMM, too, had got several bonded labourers including children released in these States. The Sub-Divisional Magistrates in these 13 States refused to give release-certificates to the freed labourers[12], because it goes against their own affidavit of 1995. The BMM took this case to the Supreme Court, which, instead of pronouncing a Judgement, appointed a Commission to enquire about the authenticity of the affidavit. The Commission is headed by a High Court Judge and has members from voluntary organisations of these 13 States. BMM's help is also sought in 6 of the States where it has its Units. The overall coordination is being done by the General Secretary of BMM. The Chief Secretaries of the government of these 13 States have been given the power to file cases of bonded labourers. However, the BMM is not satisfied with all this. It wants that the Supreme Court should have pronounced some Judgement in the case. BMM has handed over the case of rehabilitation of released workers to the NHRC, which, however, does not have any judicial powers.

On asking whether BMM had to face any bureaucratic delays in getting registered as a Society or in getting the FCRA registration, General Secretary's response was that for a genuine organisation, these are not difficult tasks. However, BMM acquired FCRA in 1994 after 13 years of its establishment. It was revealed that till 1994, BMM was a member of an independent Trust called "Mukti Pratishthan", that used to disburse funds for release and rehabilitation of bonded workers. The Trust had been registered under FCRA. In 1993, two of the trustees were found embezzling funds and a case was registered against them. This state of affairs led the BMM to part the company with the Trust and apply for an independent FCRA registration.

The General Secretary informed that with the Income Tax Department BMM had no problems. The returns are filed by the Chartered Accountant after Annual Auditing.

The General Secretary of BMM felt that the Government should work with the NGOs. The BMM invites important political leaders to its meetings and seminars. It was instrumental in getting all the major political parties to include the issue of child labour in their election manifestoes.

9. BMM and the Police

BMM, due to the nature of its work is in constant need of the cooperation of police officials. In conducting raids to locate bonded labourers and get them released and in solving several other problems of the workers, the cooperation of the police becomes essential. The police are often cooperative but occasionally side with the employers, who are the influential people in the area. For instance, the BMM, in 1990, had mobilised the striking stone quarry workers of Sohna, Gurgaon, who were demanding provision of minimum wages. The employers, who were politically influential, held the BMM responsible for the strike and according to the General Secretary, bribed the police to carry out a physical assault on him. According to the General Secretary, even the local authorities, District Collectors and Sub-Divisional Magistrates could not protect him because they were afraid of the powerful politicians and the vested interests.

10. Strategy of Putting Pressure on Government

The Chairperson of the BMM, Swami Agnivesh, elaborates his strategy of working for the abolition of child labour thus:

> "The pressure we intend to apply on the government is essentially a democratic pressure, pressure of the public opinion and that is why we have been organising marches, seminars, issuing press statements and criticising the government for lack of commitment or political will. Still there is very little awareness. That is where the Government is proving to be unmindful and immune to criticism. The present Government's (BJP Government in March 1999) situation is very unstable because they are trying to survive on a day to day basis. Every second or third day, there is some kind of crisis and we do not know when they will have that amount of stability so that they can really address the basic problems facing the country. In this connection, I would not say as part of our pressure strategy but as part of our lobbying strategy, I met the Prime Minister especially on this issue and tried to convince him that child labour problem and education for this segment of population who are in bondage should be given the top-most priority. I even suggested that the Prime Minister should allot to himself the portfolio of Human Resource Development so that the message goes across to the whole government and to everyone else that this government means business. Prime Minister's response was very favourable. To further it, I do not see any step being taken except for a small enhancement in the budgetary allocation by the Finance Minister, which does not hold much of a hope".

11. Future of Child Bonded Labourers and Role of NGOs

According to Swami Agnivesh, with the present complacent attitude of the Government, the future of children who are in bondage is very bleak. He thinks that the government is not serious about its commitment to make elementary education for all children a fundamental right. He also realises that it is extremely difficult and challenging to mobilise resources to meet the goal of compulsory universal primary education for children.

In this context, Swami Agnivesh considers the role of NGOs to be identification, release and rehabilitation of child labourers using the law of the land and the resources provided by the government. He wants the NGOs to also highlight the problem obtaining at the macro-level by spreading critical awareness in the society. NGOs should go to the root of the problem by making the parents of bonded children aware of the evils of child labour.

12. Role of BMM in Social Transformation

In the words of Swami Agnivesh:

> "Our organisation from the very beginning has tried to analyse every exploited situation in terms of social change. As activists, we have tried to challenge the caste system, the fatalistic attitude towards life, communalism, which divides the poor, conspicuous lack of accountability and have asked for transparency at the Government level. Our organisation, very often has to resist some negative changes taking place in the wider society, e.g., reckless liberalisation, indiscriminate globalisation that is taking place in the wider society. For doing this, we network with organisations and movements of a wide ranging variety but which have a lot of commonality in perspective. That is how we are a part of the National Alliance of the People's Movement. BMM is also closely related with a 125 years old social reform movement called Arya Samaj".

13. Educational Activities of BMM

The following account is based on our field visits, from December 1998 till June 1999, to the 8 Schools in Faridabad, 1 in Delhi and a vocational-cum-educational centre in Faridabad, and interviews with the field workers, teachers and children.

13.1 Schools in Faridabad

These schools are located in and around the stone quarries of Faridabad.

It is a unique step to open schools in such far-flung and remote areas. The Government has certain parameters (demographic), regarding opening of schools and cannot open schools in such area unless there is at least 80 students. But NGOs have flexibility, they can go to a neglected area according to their own ethics and start their projects. The children studying here are either working in the stone quarries themselves or their parents were bonded labourers. Both the children and their parents were released and rehabilitated by the BMM and a colony for them was established with water and electric supply, ration shops, medical facility and non-formal full time school for children. In the absence of the school these children would have accompanied their parents to the stone quarries and rendered their services in various operations like removal of dust, carrying of small stones etc.

There are eight such schools in Faridabad, viz., Jaswant Dera, Mehtaru Dera, Dhurva Dera, Pali 1, Pali 2, Manger, Lohari 1 and Lohari 2. The schools impart non-formal education for two-three years. The aim is to inculcate the habit of going to school among the children so that after completing their studies here they may join a regular school. Out of these eight schools, two viz., Mehtaru Dera and Dhurva Dera, have been taken over by the Haryana Government. In the Pali region of Faridabad, there are three schools and in Mangar there is one school. Two schools are in the Sohna region, viz., Jaswant Dera and Babulal Dera. The basic qualification for a teacher for these schools is at least Matriculation. A brief account of some of these schools is as follows:

13.1.1 Mehtaru Dera School

It is a Primary School being run jointly by BMM and Haryana Government. BMM has appointed a teacher who is being paid by its funds, while the Haryana Government has provided two teachers to the school. The children totalling 115 are in the age range of 6-11 years. Their class-wise distribution is as follows:

Class I	60 children	Boys outnumbered girls in enrolment.
Class II	28 children	
Class III	13 children	
Class IV	14 children	

The children belong to backward and scheduled castes. Some of them are Muslims and Christians. The school was started in the year 1987-88 when BMM gathered 30-40 children into one small building (one room) constructed especially for this purpose. With time the number of children increased, so BMM approached the Haryana Government for a school building. Thus, the Government built a two-room school building and provided with two teachers.

The children are being provided with books, slates, rug-cloth flooring (on which children sit in the classroom). Uniforms are provided for children who join in Class I and biscuits are given to all children. The biscuits are distributed so that the children have motivation for attending to school.

13.1.2 Dhurva Dera School: A Success Story

The Dhurva Dera School was set up by the BMM for children of the bonded labourers released by it. Initially, the attendance in the school was too low and the parents and children were to be motivated to come to the school by giving uniforms and biscuits. With time these very former bonded labourers started working in the nearby factories and hence now have an enhanced economic status. They, therefore, realise the importance of education and schooling with the result more and more children got enrolled in the school. Inspired by the success of the Dhurva Dera School, it was taken over completely by the Haryana Government. BMM does not provide any teacher or any incentives, not even biscuits here since all the children are going to School. This, therefore, may be counted as a success story of the BMM.

13.1.3 Lakkadpura School at Kattanpahari, Sohna, Faridabad

It is a one-room school with one teacher who is a matriculate. There are around 30 children. The teacher is free to decide about what to teach and how. The books are based on the syllabus of Haryana Government Schools. No child among them was a worker in the stone quarries though their parents work in the quarries. One of the pupils had earlier worked in a *dhaba* for a brief period.

13.1.4 Mohan Dera School

It is a unique School, as it has not been established by BMM but by the residents of the Mohan Dera. This settlement is of former bonded labourers who were rescued and provided this permanent space for dwelling due to the efforts of BMM. The children of this settlement till February 1999 were going to the Mehtaru Dera School. But in order to reach there, they had to cross a busy road with heavy trucks plying on them. The residents, therefore, decided to have a school at the settlement area itself. It is situated on a small piece of land without any shelter and the children brave the chilly winters and the hot summers out in the open. In the rainy season they do not attend the school. The residents arranged the teacher for this school itself. The school runs between 8 a.m. to 1 p.m. with 45 children. It is a primary school. The parents work in the stone quarries but do not want their children to join them there and instead want them to be educated so that they are aware of their rights and cannot be exploited by others. The residents arranged for notebooks since this school is not being funded by any agency. More surprising is the fact that even the Chairperson did not know about the existence of this school at the time when the authors conducted field visits there!

The day the authors visited the school, all the residents of the Mohan Dera had taken a day off since they planned to lay the foundation of this school. The field worker who has a direct contact with the Secretariat was informed about it and in his presence they dug up the place for the school building. The fact that parents had taken leave from their work and sacrificed one day's wage, showed how keen they were to educate their children. The need of the hour now is to provide quality education to the children.

This case dramatically demonstrates the efficacy of the BMM strategy and its emphasis on awareness. It is due to the efforts of Swami Agnivesh's magic words to the workers on to arise and to snatch away what is due to them, that the workers have become so conscious about the need for education for their children.

13.1.5 Pali School No. 1

This school is being sponsored by ILO-IPEC. It is a small, one-room building accommodating 40 children. The age of the children ranges from 6 to 10 years. The older children either go to the government school or just while away their time. Girl children take care of cooking responsibilities and look after their younger siblings in the home. Hence the attendance is low in the school. One of the teachers there had done a diploma course in Pharmacy. He was practising in a slum in Delhi but when the municipal authorities asked the residents of the slum to vacate the area, he came to Pali where his relatives were working in the stone quarry. There he met a field worker of the BMM who was on look out for a teacher for this school and as such recruited him. As he was new to this field, he did not know what to teach and there was no body to guide him.

The basic problem in the Faridabad schools for the wards of the stone quarry workers is that these children go away with their parents to their villages in the agricultural seasons and not all of them come back. Those who come back forget whatever was taught during their long break. Another point to be mentioned here is that the parents send their children with great hopes since they believe that their children should be educated enough to find some decent jobs and should not, like them, break stones. However, the standard of education is such that it encourages rote learning and only makes children barely literate. At the same time the teachers have not been given the responsibility to get the children admitted to government schools once they complete their 5-year non-formal full time education. As such, the teachers do, not know what happens to children who pass out of the school. This shows that the BMM is not able to not pay much attention to the quality of education, which is mainly due to lack of funds. The grant making agencies budget the salaries of teachers to Rs 1,000-1,500, hence BMM has to make do with untrained teaching staff who, in turn fail to make much of a difference to their students lives.

13.1.6 Establishing Schools: Some Stories

The field worker of BMM visits the worker's colony in the stone quarries of Faridabad to find out the total number of children in that area and whether they were going to government schools (which is far off). If a large number of children are out of the school, he would speak to the parents and encourage them to send their children to the school, which they would then soon establish. The field workers also try to find out from that area itself some one qualified enough to teach children. Then the relevant authorities are approached for acquisition of the land for school and for building a one-room structure. Sometimes, a school is started in any sheltered space till the building is constructed. For instance, in Pali area of Faridabad, a cowshed is being temporarily being used for school. The school building is under construction nearby. If there is an existing structure lying unused and which has space to accommodate the school, then permission of the owner is sought for its use. This happened in case of the vocational-cum-educational centre. Swami Agnivesh approached the Arya Gurukul in Faridabad for seeking permission to use one of their annexes and on getting permission managed to establish a school for about 40 boys.

13.2 Vocational-cum-Educational Centre

The BMM has embarked on a unique programme titled 'Integrated Ameliorative Programme for Bonded and Child Labour', a multi-faceted programme in Faridabad, Haryana. The aim of the programme as stated in its Annual Report, 1998-1999 is technical training combined with social and cultural development for ex-bonded and child labour in the age group of 13-14 years, with 6 months training for the acquisition of skills. The trainees after completion of their training can set up their own establishments to lead a life of human dignity. Stress is laid on imparting training in such trades that have the potential of becoming family occupations and other unemployed persons in the family can also join the venture. It will help in raising the social and economic status of the family.

The Vocational Centre is housed in Gurukul, Faridabad – a well laid out structure with lush green sprawling lawns. The Centre is exclusively for boys. The boys coming here have never been to any school and were earlier engaged in some kind of work in garages or in the quarries. During the time of fieldwork, the first batch of students were being trained. Free boarding and lodging is provided to the trainees. When the authors visited the Centre in December 1998, there were 17 boys in this programme. They were learning trades like carpentry and tailoring. These are trades that are much in demand both in rural and semi-urban areas.

Apart from vocational training, non-formal education is also being provided, the aim being to give primary education in one year. Along with these, the boys are also taught yoga for good physical and mental health. The principles of Arya Samaj like equality of human beings, fighting against injustice, alcoholism is also inculcated in the children. Their daily routine is as follows:

The boys have to get up at 4 a.m., do yoga and other exercises and practice what was taught the previous day, this can go on till 8 a.m. Breakfast is served between 8 a.m. to 9 p.m. Studies and training go on till 12 p.m., when lunch is served. Then the boys take rest for one hour. But for another two hours i.e. from 2 p.m. to 4 p.m., they again have to gear themselves for studies. From 4 p.m. to 5 p.m., yoga is taught to them. From then on they can play any game for about an hour. There is an open piece of land nearby for them to play. After that, they revise whatever has been taught, complete their homework and have dinner and go to bed at 9 p.m. sharp.

Although, the Gurukul can accommodate 25 boys, there were only 17 boys at the time of research. The boys here were a really happy lot. They liked the sheltered life with free boarding and lodging facility, free meals and even exclaimed that the teacher here gives the love and affection equivalent to their parents. They were hopeful that they would have a secure future. However, since this centre is located in the compounds of Arya Gurukul, the teachers of Gurukul make fun of these boys by calling them "bandhua mazdoor" (bonded labourers). The boys take bath in the nearby stream from where the Gurukul people hush them away. Even the houses where their parents live, is the property of Gurukul. Its Management threatens their parents with lathis for not paying any rent for the last 6-7 years. However, the fault lies partly with the parents, since the rent is very minimal, just Rs. 20 per year. The children asked the authors to talk to Swami Agnivesh about it and get the amount written off. This apart, the children have no problems and are free and happy here.

13.3 Samata School

BMM, despite its primary activities namely liberation of bonded and child labour and their rehabilitation, has planned to take up the amelioration of the down-trodden and the neglected segments of the society living in the slums. Hence, it has set up an education centre in the slums of Garhi, Delhi. Its aims and objectives are:

1. To wean working children away from their work and ensure that those not working do not take to work by inducting them in informal schools. Those who exhibit their talent and aptitude in studies can join in a school of formal education later.
2. Since education does not figure in the list of priorities of these poor people, the school aims at sensitising parents about the need to educate children to free them from the trap of poverty.
3. To create a better future for the girl children. They have either to look after domestic chores or accompany their mothers engaged in house-hold work to lend a helping hand. (Quite a number of girls in the Garhi slum, have taken up jobs as part time workers in homes, sweeping floors, washing utensils and the like).

The story of the establishment of the school goes like this. The Municipal Corporation of Delhi allotted the first floor of the Community Centre at the Garhi slum to BMM. Initially, it was planned to be a Branch Office of the BMM Secretariat. However, Swami Agnivesh felt that since it was difficult for him to manage even one office with the funds he receives, another office would be too much of a burden. On visiting the slum, an insight into the socio-economic status of the inhabitants was gained. Most of the inhabitants were working as domestic workers, auto-rickshaw drivers, casual labourers in Municipalities or were engaged in other menial jobs. Their children either went with their mothers to work as domestic help or whiled away their time. Very few of them went to the government school nearby. Some were overage to gain admission in Class I in the regular schools. Hence, it was decided to open a school at the allotted space in the Community Centre. A Graduate worker, who worked as caretaker of the Community Centre agreed to teach the children. But since the school is not included in a project, there is no funding for it. Efforts were made by volunteers to make it a project and submit it to an international agency. However, no international agency gives funds for a project with such a small budget. Lack of funding comes in the way of the smooth functioning of the school. Children were promised free notebooks, books, pencils, slates, etc. But after some time when the first lot of notebooks donated by the South African volunteer was exhausted, there were many problems in buying new sets. The system went haywire. The teacher asked children to buy their own books. The Director was reported of it and another set was purchased, but it appears that till some funds are committed, the school will have a precarious existence.

In order to attract all the children, even those who were going out to work in the morning hours, the timing of the school had been adjusted and till June 1999, the school used to work between 2 p.m. to 5 p.m. Later, seeing that this practice only regularises child labour, the timings were changed to 8 a.m. to 2 p.m. This has caused working children to drop out. The strength of the school has come down from 50-55 to about 25 children. But this is only a transitional phase. The children, who have left do want to study, but in the afternoon hours. One of the boys, who lives with his Uncle, is waiting for his parents to arrive from Nepal so that he could quit work and attend the school. Thus, what is clear is that there is a growing interest among the children as well as the parents in the slum to go to school.

14. Some Case Studies of Beneficiary Children

14.1 Sarva Singh: Sarva Singh is an 11 years old boy studying in Class III in Lakkadpura School at Kattanpahari, Faridabad. He is the eldest among his two brothers and two sisters. He worked in a *dhaba* (roadside restaurant) in a nearby township for two months. His father was a Foreman in Sohna and earned a decent amount. His parents were ignorant about the value of education and hence had sent him off to work so that he may do something in his life. He did not complain of ill treatment by his employer whose children also worked in the *dhaba.* Yet, he decided to quit work because he could get no time to rest and play. The customers were insensitive and unconcerned about him and kept asking him to do something or the other. It was only at night that he got time to take rest but again he had to get up early in the morning to clean the place. However, Sarva Singh left his job when he got ill and returned home. After he recovered, his parents admitted him in this school along with his younger siblings. He believes that if he studied he would be "somebody" when he grows up. He looked very mature for his age and he kept his eyes downcast while narrating his work experience in the *dhaba* showing that he was ashamed of the fact that he had worked and thus had developed a low self-esteem.

14.2 Amarjit Kumar: Amarjit Kumar is 14 years old and is undergoing training in carpentry and tailoring in the Gurukul Indraprastha. His father works in a factory and mother in the stone quarry. He belongs to scheduled caste family and hails from Madhya Pradesh. The family income is around Rs. 2,500 per month. Amarjit used to live in the village but did not like to study in the school since his teacher used to scold too much. He left the school after three years and came to live with his parents in Faridabad. Here, he started working in a garage from morning till evening earning Rs. 200-300 per month. A *Vaidya* (Doctor) of the Arya Gurukul told his father about the Vocational-cum-educational Centre who in turn admitted Amarjit in the Centre. It was hoped that on getting trained in a particular craft, Amarjit would be a skilled worker and would have a better future. Amarjit likes the homely and sheltered atmosphere of the Centre and is enjoying his stay here.

14.3 Mahan: Mahan is 11-year-old boy from Nepal. He lives in the slum of Garhi, Delhi. His father is a *Chowkidar* (guard) and mother maid servant and they have to feed five children. Mahan is the eldest of the siblings. He works in an office as a cleaner boy for three hours a day in the mornings and earns Rs. 250 per month. He started coming to the Samata School, which, initially operated, from 2 p.m. to 5 p.m. However, since July 1999, the school started operating in the morning hours, making it impossible for Mahan to attend. He wants the teacher to teach him in the afternoons or evenings, but the teacher has his other preoccupations. When interviewed, Mahan said that when his parents come back from Nepal (they had gone there for agricultural reasons), he would leave his job and resume his schooling.

14.4 Vijay: Vijay belongs to Meerut (Uttar Pradesh) and is 12 years old. He has five younger brothers and an elder brother. His parents who belong to the backward caste, came to Delhi 15 years ago. They first worked in NOIDA and Vijay studied till Class II there. They then came to Garhi slum and for some time Vijay just used to roam about. Then he started working as a domestic help in the Kailash Colony, nearby, earning Rs. 800 per month. Whatever he had studied in the school at NOIDA, he soon forgot. When Samata School started in Garhi in December 1998, he gradually got interested in the school because he did not like his work. He joined the school from February 1999 and has progressed well in the school.

14.5 Chaturlal: Chaturlal studies in Class IV in the Mohan Dera School, Faridabad. He is 11 years old and has two sisters and two brothers, he is the eldest among them. He is originally from Khagaria village, Bihar. His parents came here 20 years back. His father breaks stones and his mother clears the mud (from where the stones are dug) in the stone quarry and they get respectively, Rs. 60 and Rs. 50 per working day. His parents own land and house in the village and go there seasonally. Chaturlal studied till Class II in the village before coming to Faridabad. Here he used to while away his time, till this school was started by the residents of Mohan Dera, who work in the stone quarry and have been unionised by the efforts of BMM. This school has not yet been funded by any agency and hence the workers buy books and other stationary from their own money. Chaturlal is a regular student and said that he likes to study.

Several more of the children in the schools run by BMM in Faridabad were interviewed, all of whom exhibited certain basic social attributes. Their parents either belonged to the scheduled castes or, to the other backward classes, and worked in the stone quarries and all had 4-5 siblings. They came either from Madhya Pradesh or Bihar, their parents owned land and houses in the village, all of them go to their villages in the agricultural seasons and come back during the lean seasons to Faridabad to work as daily wagers. Since the children keep coming and going to their villages with some not even returning, they forget whatever they learnt and hence had to repeat their lessons. Children were not happy with the school environment, which was very hot in summers and too cold in winters. Yet, they braved bad weather conditions and came to study.

15. Future Plans

According to Swami Agnivesh, BMM plans to heighten the momentum of people's movement for education purpose and to bring in as many NGOs and religious groups as possible around this issue with a sense of commitment. In his own words, "let us all join hands to create a tremendous public pressure on the government so that education — good, relevant, quality education on the basis of equity — becomes one of the top most priorities of the Government and the society". BMM is now trying to interact and launch some sort of a loose coalition with people in the field of religion and its newly formed sister organisation, 'Religion for Social Justice' is slowly moving in this direction. The religious organisations wield tremendous clout, they have tremendous hold over the minds of the people and they are also well resourced so once it gets a good response — positive response — from the religious organisations, the organisation will be far more effective than the type of forum it has with the NGOs. BMM also plans to combine the South Asian NGO Forum with the Religious Forum for Social Justice, in this way to the whole of the civil society. In course of time, it would like to have some sort of a liaison or coalition with the local self-government (*Panchayat* system). The whole of the network — local self-government and the NGO Forum and the Religious Forum — can work together for ushering in a new era where children are fully guaranteed their right to childhood, it should meet education with the concept of 'Neighbourhood Schools', on the basis of equity and things like that. So, the organization is hopeful in course of time, this goal could be achieved, at least the network between those three different sectors could be established in an effective manner and that itself will have a tremendous impact on the policies of the Government and their priorities.

16. Achievements

On asking Swami Agnivesh the factors responsible for making the organisation successful, he said:

> "We do not think that we are a successful organisation because the tasks, which we have taken and goals set by us, are nowhere near accomplishment. Although, we have been able to release nearly one lakh and seventy thousand bonded labourers and seven

thousand child bonded labourers, yet the problem persists and is perpetuating itself. Our only success has been in creating critical awareness all around in this society, at national and international levels through the cooperation we have received from some committed journalists, lawyers and Judges of Supreme Court of India[13] , which we greatly acknowledge".

As listed in one of the documents of BMM, its achievements are:

1. It is pioneer organisation in the area of deliverance from slave like lives of nearly 1,25,000 bonded labourers from various sectors of the economy through direct actions and legal course. A large number of them have been rehabilitated. From the carpet industry alone about 10,000 children held in captivity by loom owners were rescued and reverted to their native place.
2. In the area of social evils it has raised voice against atrocities on women, child marriage, religious bigotry and communal frenzy, injustice to *dalits,* backward classes, tribals etc. and called for provision of free primary education for children upto the age of 14 with the incentive of 1 k.g. cereal for each child for each day of schooling as a food security to the families.
3. An awareness programme against the child labour system and other forms of slavery, demanding free and compulsory education to the children upto the age of 14 years was undertaken in the States of Uttar Pradesh, Maharashtra and Karnataka in the year 1996-1997 and 1997-1998. It generated a good amount of awareness among the people, parents and children. Besides, it sensitised the administration to deal with this menace effectively.
4. A South Asian Seminar on Bonded Child Labour, the first of its kind was organised in New Delhi on 30th November-1st December 1996. In it, delegates from Pakistan, India, Nepal, Sri Lanka and Bangladesh participated. A Delhi Statement by the people of South Asia on the elimination of bonded and child labour was issued.

This apart, BMM has been running directly and as a catalyst for associate organisations, a number of schools for ex-child labour in different sectors in some States.

17. Limitations

1. *Financial and Manpower Constraints*: BMM has to constantly struggle for finances and due to shortage of funds it is not able to run its projects effectively. It is forced to give meager salary to its staff, teachers and field workers who are very much dissatisfied. There is a lack of committed workers. On getting better opportunities they leave the organisation. Therefore, BMM is constrained by financial and manpower resources.
2. *Political Constraint*: The mission of BMM to eliminate child labour is constrained by the lack of political will. Political Parties, interested in vote banks, do not pay heed the problem of child labour. The Government does not totally ban child labour nor does it implement the legislation for child labour effectively. The last comprehensive Act on child labour talked of protection and regulation and not of banning it. Their task is also made difficult by the fact that the politicians have a close nexus with the employers and hence try to protect them. The political bosses nurture mafias and muscle power.

Swami Agnivesh is an internationally known figure and his views on child labour, its causes and solution have a great value. The organisation is clear about what constitutes child labour and has through it own method calculated the magnitude of child labour population in India[14]. This is something unique since most of the NGOs surveyed during this study were not clear on the question of 'who is a child labour?' Those NGOs, which are working for education of slum children, did not realise that they in a way helping in prevention and perpetuation of child labourers. Because, broadly any child not going to the school is bound to become a child labour. Unlike BMM, these NGOs are only engaged in protection of child labourers or the potential child labourers as is evident from the next chapter.

REFERENCES

1. Swami Agnivesh, founder and Chairperson of BMM, organised a protest fast by child labourers at Rajghat on 13th August, 1998 where a memorandum including a Charter of Demands was presented to the President. The Charter of Demands included:

   a. Enforcement of free and compulsory elementary education to ensure that all children under the age of 14 avail themselves of quality education based on a curriculum which is socially relevant and pedagogically sound and stimulating. The Government rather than the poor parents should assume responsibility for implementing this. Urgent steps must be insisted to establish community managed Schools where such facilities are not available. All Schools, including the existing formal ones, should be run on the model of neighbourhood Schools.

   b. Given the nexus between poverty and child labour, the parents of child labourers should be covered by National Minimum Wage (NMW) norms on par with Government Class IV employees. They should be guaranteed at least 240 days of employment at National Minimum Wage level. This is justified by Article 23 of our Constitution.

   c. All means of mass communication, particularly the Doordarshan and Akashwani should disseminate all aspects of NMW in all languages and dialects on regular basis and entertainingly through folk art and music. This will empower the voiceless and unorganised labour to galvanise and unionise themselves and fight for a rightful place in society. The resources of the mass media should also be used effectively to raise public awareness concerning the evil of child labour and to motivate the parents and the community at large to help all children under 14 to attend Schools, specially the girl children.

   d. Both Governments and the civil society should be galvanised to abolish the abominable caste system and fatalistic attitudes and socio-religious customs, which tend to perpetuate gender inequity.

   e. Last, but not least, implementation of TOTAL PROHIBITION is a must to eradicate poverty and child labour. (Article 47 of Indian Constitution).
2. *The Hindustan Times*, November 16, 1995.
3. "Of Human Bondage", *The Evening News*, Monday, February 9, 1987.
4. "Marx, Mahatma and Mantras", *Indian Express*, Sunday, February 12, 1995.
5. "The Man in the News/ Swami Agnivesh", *The Telegraph*, Saturday, April 23, 1988.
6. "Man in the News" – Swami Agnivesh, *The Telegraph*, Saturday, April 23, 1988.
7. Source: Brochure, BMM.
8. "Child Slavery and Unemployment", *The Economic Times*, May 15, 1995.
9. "Swami Agnivesh: The Monk, His Designer Sweater and the Issue of Bonded Labour", *Sunday Observer*, 17-23 January 1993.

10. Not the true name.
11. Source: BMM Annual Report, 1998-99.
12. Release-certificate is the necessary first step in the initiation of rehabilitation measures for freed bonded labourers.
13. They include Justice V.R. Krishna Ayyar, Justice P.N. Bhagwati and Advocates such as Govind Mukhoty, Krishna Mahajan, Sujit Bhattacharya, Ranjit Kumar, Fally Nariman, etc.
14. BMM's definition, causes and solution of child labour as also the role of NGOs have already been spelt out earlier in this Chapter.

6

NGO—Salaam Baalak Trust
Shelter and Education

Salaam Baalak Trust (SBT) was found to be an excellent example of an organisation engaged in protection and rehabilitation of street and working children. It is also an example of how an organisation developed out of a 'commitment to do something' for street and working children by a small group of people associated with the making of the film '*Salaam Bombay*' — a film made on street children of Bombay in 1988. SBT illustrates how the passion to cover more and more population of street and working children led to taking up a number of interrelated responsibilities such as (a) setting up of more Shelter Homes; (b) initiating community works in slums adjacent to the railway tracks to prevent children dwelling in the slums from ending up joining the labour force; (c) starting AIDS awareness programme; and (d) opening up of a residential school. The area of operation of SBT and its activities is in and around the New Delhi Railway Station.

Initially the Trust was catering to 25 boys with its 3-4 hours programme of non-formal education, theatrical art and some recreational activities. SBT has been evolving and reinventing itself with time. However, according to the Trustee, there has not been any major policy change. For instance, the focus of its work has remained over the years as the street children. But, over the years with the experience gained from dealing with street and working children of the New Delhi Railway Station and coming to know the problems such children face, SBT has expanded into interrelated areas such as working in the slums near the railway station where children just loiter around and their parents are unconcerned about their well being. It has also taken up the AIDS awareness programme for the street and working children. The street children are often sexually exploited and they know nothing about safe sexual behaviours. They are thus, prone to AIDS and other sexually transmitted diseases.

Thus, the expansion of SBT within a decade of its establishment, has overridden the desire and understanding of the founder and the Chairperson of the Trust, Ms. Praveen Nair, to remain a small set up. In her own words: "We do not want to enlarge to such an extent that we loose sight and become bureaucratic and administrative, because as the project expands, it requires more time and resources".

1. History and Progress

SBT's history as printed in its Brochure and other literature is as follows:

> "The Salaam Baalak Trust was set up after the landmark success of the film made on street children of Bombay 'Salaam Bombay' in 1980s...The film very simply but powerfully portrayed the lives of street children, their traumas and their psyche. The film left an impact of a more lasting nature on a small group of people associated with its making who had decided to come together to form a social welfare organisation that could cater to millions of such children in Delhi, Bombay (now called Mumbai) and Bhuvaneswar — the Salaam Baalak Trust. The Trust has come a long way hence and the New Delhi Centres alone cater to a population of nearly 1500 street and working children through 7 of its Learning Centres in and around the New Delhi Railway Station."

A very interesting account of the history of SBT as narrated by its founder and Trustee, Ms. Nair is as follows:

According to Ms. Nair, in the late 1980s she was not doing much of social work because of ill health till her daughter made the film "Salaam Bombay" on street children. She was greatly moved by the plight of street and working children. In her own words: "*Through the experiences with the street children and after seeing the tremendous talent of these children so much so that one of those boys got the National Award for the Best Child Artist, I got down to thinking of doing something for such children to provide long term services not only to the children who acted in the film but also to the street children, in general*". That is how SBT was started and was registered as a Charitable Trust in December 1988. But even before its registration, Ms. Nair and her group of friends from the Theatre Action Group had already started working in Delhi, Bhuvaneswar and Mumbai. These include Barry John, Dinaz Stafford, Inderjit Khurana and the present Co-Trustee, Sanjoy Roy. According to the founder, it was the groups' commitment to do something for the street and working children, that made them work together and turn their dream into reality. The initial finances for the organisation came from the Premier Show of the movie "*Salaam Bombay*" in the cities of Delhi, Bombay and Calcutta.

The founder along with the core group from the Theatre Action Group began their work despite the discouragement of their friends and others, who used to say:

> "*What are you doing? You are just striking your head against the wall. There are millions of them. How can you do it?*" Ms. Nair and her friends would reply thus: "*We do not claim to have set out to change the world, we would be satisfied if we are successful in bringing 3-4 boys out of the 25 boys we are currently working into the mainstream society*".

They also faced difficulty in dealing with street boys since such children do not easily trust others because the kinds of sufferings they have undergone. They feel that the people who have come to reform them are just another tool to involve them in drug trafficking or police harassment or taking them to some Children's Homes/Juvenile Homes.

It took the founders some 6-8 week's time to build rapport with the street and working children of the New Delhi Railway Station. The process involved walking around the railway station and making contact with them. Eventually they were successful in getting together a group of 25 boys with whom they started with some fun programmes at the Station premises for 3-4 hours. At that time, no fixed programme schedule was schedule. The aim was to first build a rapport with the children. Apart from playing a few fun games, the founders talked to the children about their work, their family, their homes and their villages, so that the children open up with them. Children were taken out for picnics, were given paper, pencils, coloured pens to draw and stories were told to them. Later, when the children became friendly, activities such as vocational training in Theatrical art as well as non-formal education programme were initiated.

After working for a couple of years the founder and her colleagues realised that whatever efforts were made in this regard were futile since the boys still got back to the same environment. This necessitated the setting up by the founding members of a Shelter Home. The Home was started in the accommodation provided by the DDA Community Centre in Chandiwali Gali of Paharganj. The same also houses the office of the SBT, which coordinates all its other centres. The Shelter Home was at that time a "hotchpotch" arrangement, since it catered to both boys and girls of all age groups. Problems developed because of keeping together boys and girls at the same Shelter Home and it was decided to have the Shelter Home converted exclusively for boys. The girl children, from then onwards were sent to those government and non-government agencies which catered to the needs of the uncared for girl children. At the same time, keeping together the young and the older boys in the same Shelter Home also led to problems, such as the older boys dominating over the younger ones. This necessitated SBT to start a 24 hour Drop-in-Shelter where the older boys — 15 years onwards — could come and go anytime at their will, could avail the facility of bathing, non-formal education, counselling and vocational training.

2. The Founder

The founder, Ms. Nair's interest in the social work dates back to the 1940s when she was 16 years of age. She belonged to a wealthy family with large house and numerous servants. The servants' children, around 15 of them, used to loiter around with no parental guidance, no schooling, no values and no life-skills. They were expected to ultimately follow their parent's occupation. Moved by their plight, she started teaching those children for 2 hours, which she found a very satisfying experience. The parents of the servant's children started questioning her as to why she was teaching them, since they would never be able to rise from the lowest rung of the socio-economic hierarchy. So it was a challenge for her to enlighten their parents and also a challenge as to not "rock the boat" in their family situation. Ms. Nair used her influence to get those boys part-time jobs of ball pickers at a tennis court. To the girls, she taught some arts and crafts like painting and stitching. This is how she started her tenure in social works.

3. Philosophy/Objectives

SBT's objective is to bring about a difference in street and working children's life and try and integrate them into the mainstream, as also to give them the childhood, which they have totally lost because they have to earn their living at a tender age. According to Ms. Nair, the organisational philosophy is to focus on the quality of services provided tc a child and not to the number of children covered.

The basic objectives of SBT are as under[1] :

a) To provide basic literacy and provide facility for those children who wish, to study further
b) To provide health, recreational and counselling services to street children
c) To provide for and encourage street children to develop their potential by providing creative opportunities
d) To provide facilities whereby street children may be reunited with their families where possible
e) To propagate healthy living and sanitation amongst street children
f) To make available a secure space where street children can play and enjoy what remains of their childhood
g) To instill public awareness and respect for the rights and lives of these children.

4. Organisational Structure of SBT

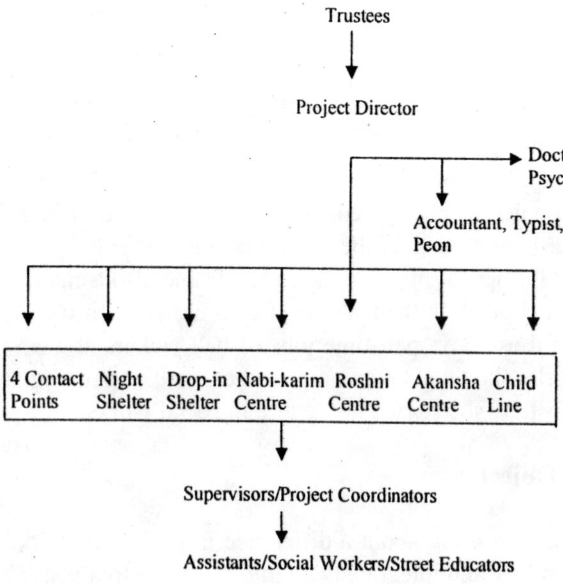

SBT started with a staff strength of 3 — a social worker, a theatre person and a health worker, which has now swelled to 50.

The top Management comprises of 2 Trustees, viz. Ms. Praveen Nair and Mr. Sanjoy Roy, who are also the founders of the organisation. They do not draw any salary. The major decisions regarding organisational policy and finances rests with the Trustees. SBT also utilises the services of a Medical Practitioner at the Safdarjung Hospital, Dr. Bittra George, who though not a Trustee, is an authorised signatory of the organisation. He also takes charge of the Trust in the absence of both the Trustees.

Next in the hierarchy is the Project Director. He supervises the staff and the working of SBT. Besides office work, he is required to conduct supervisory visits to monitor the project implementation. Among the technical staff are the accountant, the Nurse, the Project Coordinators and the Psychologist. Below them in the hierarchy are the Social Workers or the Street Educators who are out in the field educating the street and working boys as well as the slum children.

Though there is role clarity among the different positions, still overlapping of roles could be observed in certain cases. For instance, the Coordinators could be seen performing the role of Counsellor or Nursery Teacher, in the latter's absence. In fact, one of the Coordinators informed that in a social welfare organisation one cannot have clear-cut roles and one is required to perform many a roles at the same time.

4.1 Recruitment

The recruitment process consists of advertising the posts in the leading newspapers. The applications are scrutinised and candidates are interviewed. The Selection Committee comprising of Trustees and Project In-charge are involved in the whole process. Interview process is followed by field exposure of the selected candidates, who are required to make field visits of the different Centres of SBT for a week. Candidates are thereby asked about their on-field observations such as 'what is being done at the centres, what are the limitations, what more is required and what their contribution would be towards the organisation'. On the basis of their responses they are finally selected or rejected.

The Director agreed that the organisation faces the difficulty in recruiting qualified, experienced and dedicated people as also the problem of retaining the staff. On being probed about the problems that the staff faced during the course of their work, the Coordinator of Night Shelter summarised them as follows:

> "Unlike the Government functionaries, the staff in NGOs do not have any job security, since it is run by one person and work under his/her whims. There are no medical or any other facility for the staff. No care is provided to the workers. The staff in SBT is exposed to circumstances, which are detrimental to their health, e.g., the workers and staff deal with children suffering from a number of infectious diseases, they have to physically touch them and talk to them. In the field the workers are not only braving the harsh working conditions of the railway station, but also some criminal elements among the children. The lack of job security and medical care in such circumstances leads to non-commitment of the staff, who leave on getting better opportunity".

4.2 Rule Adherence

As far as the office staff is concerned, they are required to report on time. On every Saturday of the week, there is a Staff Meeting with Trustees and Director, where the work done during the week is analysed, the next week's programme is finalised and where the field staff put forth to the management material requirements for the children. In case of field staff who work with the children living and working in the railway station flexibility of time is allowed.

4.3 Decision-making

The decisions regarding policy and fundraising are taken by the Trustees. They also have the final say in the selection of candidates. However, in the day-to-day functioning of the organisation, decision-making process is participatory. Every Saturday, after 2 p.m., a staff-management meeting is held in which the Trustees encourage participation to find solutions to the problem of the staff or the beneficiary children. Also at this meeting, the staff may give their inputs/suggestions for improving the ongoing projects. Here, we may cite the case of children's excursion to Nainital in Summer Vacations (June 99). The staff in one of the Saturday meetings conveyed to the Trustees the idea to take the children to Nainital that summer. It was agreed upon and the following week, preparations began to send the children to the trip. In the meeting, the staff may also put forth their requirements, mainly of the stationary items, for the following week, which get sanctioned.

Unfortunately, meetings between the beneficiary children and the staff and management is lacking. They do not have a say in the decision-making process, and decisions regarding schemes for their own welfare are taken without consulting their view-point. Here, mention may be made of the instance of food served in the Shelter Home. One child complained to the authors that he was fed up of eating the same kind of food in the Shelter Home. Had the children been consulted before preparing the menu for the week, they would not have such kind of a grievance. This makes the case for adopting participatory approach while working with the beneficiaries.

4.4 Networks with Other Organisations

SBT networks with the NGO Forum for Street and Working Children with which regular meetings are conducted. NGO Forum for Street and Working Children is a forum for advocacy of rights of street children. It is also a pressure group for implementation of street children friendly programmes such as:

- Sensitisation of street educator
- Medical programme for street children
- Integration camp trip to Mumbai and Pune
- Training programme on HIV/AIDS for street educators

SBT is also a member of the following forums:

1. NGO AIDS Forum, part of a six member group advocating HIV/AIDS prevention programmes and upholding rights of HIV positive people
2. South Asian Fund Raising Group, which is a forum for fund raisers
3. SBT is a Coordinator of the Model HIV Counselling Centre

at Safdarjang Hospital which provides pre- and post-test counselling, after care and support services for HIV positives

4. SBT Networks with the following national and international agencies in furtherance of its goals and objectives:
   - National AIDS Control Organisation (NACO)
   - Ministry of Health and Family Welfare
   - Ministry of Women and Child Welfare
   - Human Resource Development Ministry
   - Delhi Development Authority
   - Municipal Corporation of Delhi
   - Indian Railways
   - NCERT and SCERT
   - British High Commission
   - UNAIDS
   - UNESCO
   - UNDCP
   - UNDP
   - UNICEF

SBT staff are invited to attend Seminars organised by the like-minded organisations such as Butterflies and Prayas.

4.5 Project Selection

The projects taken up by the organisation are decided on the basis of the need of the community. Here we illustrate the selection process of one of the most recent project of SBT, i.e., is the project on slum dwellers of Nabi Karim situated near the railway station. The project aims to educate the children of slums, around the railway tracks. Hence, it is a preventive programme. Before initiating any action, baseline survey was carried out and accordingly the project site was decided. The criterion used in the selection of the site was to reach a large number of beneficiaries. Also resource availability at the disposal of SBT was checked. Thereafter, community participation was sought. This included talking to the residents of the slum, Pradhan and Municipal Authorities. Women residents, who were willing, were made teachers of the proposed NFE School. A one room hut was constructed and the school, thus, started functioning.

5. Finances

The founder/Trustee of SBT informed that in the initial years fund raising used to take up much of her time. This is not the case now. She also apprised that SBT does not have any international funding such as from the UN. "Only 1/3rd or 1/4th of SBT's funding is from outside India". In her own words: "Once you start a project and people begin to recognise it as good work, funds automatically start pouring in". She gave the following account of SBT's funders:

- Grant from the Ministry of Social Justice and Empowerment for Street Children.
- Drop-in-shelter of SBT was initiated without any commitment from any organisation but one organisation — British High Commission — gave SBT some money and the shelter was started.
- One of the funding agencies, viz., Trees for Life came into SBT's contact rather accidentally. At one of the SBT Children's Programmes at the India International Centre prepared by the famous theatre personality Dadi Padamjee, a gentleman for this American organisation got very much inspired by the performance of the children and the organization. He came forward and offered funds to SBT.
- SBT's AIDS awareness and counselling programme is being funded by NACO.
- SBT also gets some foreign donations of not more than 1000 dollars in a year, which is again from individuals and not from any funding agency. And it is through people coming to SBT, seeing its work and somehow believing in it. For instance, a few years ago some visitors from Netherlands had come to Delhi to attend a Conference. They heard of SBT's work and so they called on the Trustee and expressed a wish to be taken to the different learning centres of SBT. They were much impressed by the work being done at the centres. In Netherlands, they organised a group of people and sent back some money to SBT.
- SBT also receives funds, of around Rs. 10-12 lakh per year, in terms of small donations from individuals in remitting amounts ranging from Rs. 100/- to Rs. 5000/-.

The funders require SBT to furnish details of how their money has been spent. They also make a visit to its to monitor project implementation and to see the progress of the beneficiaries. SBT submits Progress Reports every six months or whenever the donor agency asks for it. Apart from this, SBT also submits its Annual Reports to its funders.

The Director agreed that there are "strings attached in aid disbursement". According to him, getting the funds released from government departments involves numerous problems and struggles. Processing of funds take a minimum of 6 months. There are unnecessary inquiries, irrelevant questioning. The persons, deputed for the task of processing of funds, are not suitable for the post and that's why there are problems. This delay has adverse effect on the work since the workers loose enthusiasm and zeal. SBT has to sometimes make changes in its project proposal to the government since the government demands a classification between street and working children as in the government's scheme there are programmes for working children and not for the street children. Accordingly, SBT has to change its way of working. SBT wants to become self-sufficient in funding so that it does not have to depend on institutional sources for funding.

6. Activities

6.1 Keeping in line with the objectives and goals of the organisation, SBT has undertaken the following activities[2] :

6.1.1 Shelter

The younger children (aged below 14 years) from the railway station who have no anchor, are vulnerable and exposed to the vagaries of nature and anti-social elements, are provided shelter at the Night Shelter of SBT. The Night Shelter accommodates a maximum of 50 children.

6.1.2 Drop-in-Shelter

Since the Night Shelter is only for children, who are below the age of 14 years, in order to provide shelter for older children, a 24 hour Drop-in-Shelter has been initiated where in children, especially the older ones could drop in anytime, take rest, have a secure place to keep their belongings, undertake some kind of vocational training if they wished so and avail of the free medical services of SBT.

6.1.3 Health Services

Street and working children are provided basic medical assistance through a doctor, a nurse and a medical social worker. Serious cases are provided health care through various government hospitals. As a preventive measure, a nutritious supplementary snack is prepared at the base kitchen and supplied to the children. Briefly, the various health related activities are: organisation of medical camps and awareness camp; strengthening of the medical centre; early detection and treatment of diseases; health education and health promotion; immunisation programmes; provision of nutritious and supplementary snacks and meals and conducting health related surveys, collection and tabulation of data.

6.1.4 Income Generation Activities

Street and working children are taught and motivated to produce small saleable items like painted and wax filled *diyas* (lamps), greeting cards, birthday return-gift packets, decoration packets, and so on. These items made by the children are kept for sale in the annual Diwali Fete. The collections are used for children's welfare activities. The working children who earn doing various jobs are encouraged to save their money with the social workers of SBT. Proper account and records are maintained of the savings. The children are given Rs. 10 as interest for every Rs. 100 saved by them in a month. Children are also given credit for income generating programme.

6.1.5 Education

The main thrust of educational activities at the various centres of SBT has been on school enrolments. However, it has realised that the formal education system is inadequate to meet the educational needs of these children. Therefore, the basic non-formal education that initially was being provided by SBT at its centres was modified to suit and meet the educational demands at schools. SBT organised training programmes for field level functionaries and other staff members, in order to facilitate better transfer of learning and providing a multi-graded teaching environment at its centres.

6.1.6 Vocational Training

Vocational training programme of SBT includes training in screen-printing, bookbinding, music, cutting and tailoring, for the older children. For the younger children, activities such as music, paper craft and clay modelling are taught which are therapeutic in nature. Apart from its regular vocational training courses, a community polytechnic scheme of the Delhi State Government has been launched through active networking with the concerned departments. Along with the vocational training activities, children are also placed in jobs or are apprenticed where they earn and learn.

6.1.7 Recreation

Educational tours, picnics, audio-visual media, indoor and outdoor games are encouraged since they provide adequate opportunities for recreation to the street and working children and help in channelising their energies constructively. Children are also encouraged to prepare skits, songs, dances etc. for various celebrations and festivals. Theatre and puppetry workshops are organised which have proved to be of therapeutic value to the street children while providing constructive activities during leisure.

6.1.8 Counselling

SBT attempts to identify the psychological profile of the child through the CAT/TAT (psychological tests) and other tests and counselling is provided to them according to the psychic level of each child.

6.1.9 Rehabilitation

The term rehabilitation at SBT is taken to mean reuniting the working child with his family, enabling him to become self-dependent or the migration of a family from the slum cluster either to his native village or to a *pucca* (well-built) settlement. Making a street and working child self-dependent means undertaking a series of activities such as vocational training, job placement, ensuring job satisfaction and finally the child's separation from the Night Shelter into a lodging of his own which would imply rehabilitation in the society.

6.1.10 Advocacy

SBT has a well-structured programme of utilising the medium of theatre to advocate the cause of street and working children. Participatory plays are evolved and staged in public schools, other organisations and institutions. SBT has also appeared in newspapers several times and programmes have been featured in All India Radio and Television. Various functions and competitions are organised in which, people from all walks of life are invited.

6.1.11 Assistance to Families of Street Children

Counseling, medical services, family planning and income generation are some of the various forms of assistance provided to the families of street children.

6.1.12 Sponsorship Programmes

In order to mobilise funds for its corpus, SBT has three kinds of sponsorship programme – 'Sponsor a Child', 'Sponsor Income Generation Schemes', 'Make an Individual Donation'. The donations are also accepted in kind, for instance, in the form of sweaters, blankets, dry rations, toys and games, educational aids, stationery, medicines, etc.

In addition, SBT expects and appeals to the general public to spend time with its children as a counsellor, friend, teacher, or a doctor.

SBT also expects people to provide employment to its beneficiary children since, according to the organisation, these children can be successful carpenters, gardeners, tailors, artists in design studios, factory apprentices etc. But their only limitation is a lack of opportunity for them.

Recently, SBT initiated a Sponsorship Programme in close collaboration with USA based NGO. The scheme requires children to maintain a link with their sponsors through correspondence. The children also receive small interesting gifts from their sponsors like small toys, pencils, stamps, stickers, chocolates etc. and somewhat larger gifts like umbrellas and school bags.

6.2 Learning Centres

The children working at the railway station work either as illegal porters or are rag pickers, picking up iron or plastic materials and selling it off. They work in and out at this tender age when they should be studying, playing and enjoying life. They work in harsh conditions and are prone to cuts, bruises and infections. With no shelters, when they sleep, they are vulnerable to sexual exploitation by perverts. They may also get caught in the web of anti-social elements who use them for activities like thefts and drug trafficking. Such children become a victim of substance and drug abuse.

In order to bring such children to the mainstream society, to facilitate their learning process and to provide them with some recreational opportunities, SBT is running the following learning centers for their benefit.

6.2.1 Nukkad 1

Nukkad 1 is a Drop-in-Centre for all the street and working children of the railway station. It is situated amidst the hustle and bustle of the New Delhi Railway Station on platform No. 1, above GRP Police Station

6.2.2 Nukkad 2

It is located on the other side of Nukkad 1 and is a comparatively new centre and aims to serve as a catchment for children not registered at Nukkad 1. Nukkad 2, better known as Platform School, was started subsequent to the discovery that children working on the other platforms of the New Delhi Railway Station were not attending Nukkad 1 due to the fear of police, to some extent and due to the distance one has to traverse in order to get there.

6.2.3 Night Shelter

The younger children who are more vulnerable to vagaries of nature and to the anti-social elements of the Station are transferred to the

Night Shelter, which is a home for them. These children spend all their time at the Night Shelter and are dependent on SBT for all their physical, emotional and psychological needs.

6.2.4 The 24 Hour Drop-in-Shelter

The older children who, for various reasons, are compelled to work can find a secure space at the 24 hour Drop-in-Shelter. They can keep their belongings safely and can get a night's peaceful sleep. During the day, they can avail of medical services and can also take up some vocational training

6.2.5 Outreach Centres

The Outreach Centres of SBT are Akansha, Nabi Karim and Roshni situated at *Jhuggi* settlements along the railway tracks. These children are slightly fortunate since they have a shelter where they can go back and have a night's rest. Nevertheless, living conditions and other amenities need improvement, family disputes need to be resolved and interpersonal relationships need to be improved. It is these functions that the SBT centres endeavour to achieve since the organisation considers all these factors as affecting the overall development of the child.

7. SBT and the State

The activities of SBT involve protecting and rehabilitating street and working children. It does not go about conducting raids in child labour concentrated areas and holding demonstrations against child labour. Hence SBT is in a harmonious relationship with the government, although it complains of the bureaucratic delays in disbursement of funds and the like. For instance, the Director of SBT complained that they are not getting the type of cooperation that they expect from the Delhi Municipal Corporation. He gave the example of the problem of a broken wall in the office, which they wanted to be repaired. But the concerned persons were delaying the repair work by not coming when asked for. The same, according to the Director, is the case with the Sanitary and Electricity Departments.

8. Dealings with Police

Due to the nature of its interventions SBT is in continuous interaction with the police. Though, the relationship is more of cooperation, there are sometimes frictions between the two. The General Railway Police (GRP) often nabs the boys working in the railway station. The social workers talk to the police, motivate them and even show them SBT's activities for street children. Although, the police personnel at the railway station complain that these boys create problems, but they are made to realise that the street children is a major social problem and has to be dealt with sensitivity. However, police constables, who are often not highly educated, do not appreciate, understand and empathise with the objectives and intentions of the social workers. At the railway station, the terrace of GRP Police Station has been provided to the SBT where such boys come and study. During the researcher's field visits, it was a frequent sight to find the police staff asking the boys to run errands for them. Those boys being scared of the police oblige and the social workers do not intervene since they think that police are obliging them by providing the street children some space to study and play.

9. Strategy of Cooperation with the Government

With regard to the pressure SBT intends to apply on the government to solve the problem of child labour, the Chairperson's/Trustee's response was that instead of any pressure, SBT is working alongside with the Government, especially, with its Ministry of Social Justice and Empowerment. It is satisfied with 2-3 officials of this Ministry with whom it has dealings although it is not sure whether other officials, who would replace them in the time to come, will have the same level of commitment to the cause of the working children.

The Government is reviewing its own scheme for street and working children because in their scheme no provision had been kept for shelter for such children. Most NGOs are working with the slum children and not street and working children. According to the Trustee, learning from SBT's experiences, the government has realised that shelter is an important component of any programme meant for the street and working children.

The Delhi government, on realising the kind of work the NGOs are doing, is now requesting the NGOs to intervene in their Children's/ Juvenile Homes. CRY, Samarth and Prayas are doing such intervention. SBT has also been given to manage the Children's Home at Lajpat Nagar by the Delhi Administration.

According to the founder of SBT till the year 1992, Government had no programme for street children. It only had programmes for child labour and disabled children. But street children did not come under any of these categories. So the fact that the government has introduced the scheme of shelter for street children shows that the NGOs have succeeded in forming a pressure group for intended action.

10. Activities at Learning Centres

Based on the interviews with the staff and observations made on the field, the following activities were found in the different learning centres of SBT:

10.1 Night Shelter

Night Shelter is accommodated in the second floor of the DDA Community Centre in Paharganj. It caters to the educational, recreational and shelter needs of 40 run-away boys in the age group of 4-16 years. It acts as a home away from home. But there are hundreds of children at the railway station compared to which Night Shelter fulfills the needs of just a miniscule population. The boys staying here usually come from SBT's GRP contact point at the New Delhi Railway Station, where the social workers go to the platforms and persuade the errand boys to come and study at the centre. Those boys who become regular at the GRP centre are either inducted at the Night Shelter or Drop-in-Shelter depending upon their age. However, during the research it was observed that some small boys (aged between 5-10 years), who were regular at GRP centre, did not like to go to the Shelter Home because they did not like the disciplined life of the Shelter. At the same time, it was seen that some other boys (aged 8-9 years), who wanted to be in the Shelter Home but could not be accommodated there due to its limited capacity.

While most of the boys at the Shelter come through the GRP centre, with the initiation of Child Line (a free phone line service for children in distress), a number of younger boys come to the Shelter through this Child Line Free Telephone service. For instance, a 6-year-old boy was found on the street. A well wisher contacted SBT at the Child Helpline Service. At that instance SBT Child Line coordinator went to the spot and brought the boy to the Shelter Home.

Sometimes, even the police are instrumental in bringing the boys to SBT instead of taking them to the Government Remand Homes, since getting them admitted there takes lots of time due to bureaucracy prevalent there.

When a boy is brought to the Shelter he is asked about his whereabouts and reasons for leaving his home. His relatives are informed through a letter sent at the address provided by the child, which sometimes prove wrong since many a times the child does not reveal his true story. Some older children, who, on counselling agree to go back to their villages, are sent back to their homes by SBT. They are also provided with sufficient money for the journey. There are instances where parents of the run away child have come to take the child from SBT with them.

The boys follow a disciplined life at the Night Shelter and follow a set routine. They wake up at 5.30 a.m. Between 5.45 a.m. to 7 a.m., they are required to bathe and wash. They watch T.V. news till quarter past seven. Breakfast is served between 7.15 a.m. to 7.45 a.m. Those boys who are in the school going age group attend their respective schools in Paharganj. They have been admitted to either of the three Municipal Corporation run Government Schools situated there, viz. at Chuna Mandi, Chandiwali Gali, Mantola areas and also at the DAV Public School, nearby. Realising that the standard of education in Government Schools is poor, SBT is trying to get its boys admitted to a reputed public school.

The very young boys, who are to be rehabilitated or reunited with their families or who are yet to be admitted to the schools, attend class for non-formal education at the Shelter itself between 8 a.m. to 1 p.m. In the Summer/Winter Holidays, boys spend their time in Bal Bhavan, a government run institution for children, which imparts training in arts and crafts, music, martial arts, sports as well as science through practical works. The Bal Bhawan charges only a nominal fees from such children, which SBT pays for the children.

Lunch is served between 1.15 p.m. to 2.00 p.m., after which boys either take rest or are free to watch T.V. for half an hour. For the next two hours, i.e., till 4.30 p.m. they are required to study. However, there is a lack of qualified trained graduate teacher at the Night Shelter to help these children in solving their difficulties in studies. Boys are provided evening snack after which till 7 p.m. they are free, to either play, wash clothes, clean the premises, etc. The Dinner is between 7.30 p.m. to 8.30 p.m. After Dinner till 9.30 p.m., boys are required to study. From 9.30 p.m. to 10.30 p.m., they can watch T.V. or can study. They have to be in bed by 10.30 p.m. sharp.

Sleeping time is not always so peaceful for these boys. During one of our visits, children could be seen explaining themselves to the Counsellor and Coordinators. On probing, it was told that some boys, who were new entrants to the Night Shelter, had indulged in, homosexuality the following night, which was discovered by the social worker on duty. Upon questioning the children, it came to light that this kind of activity was going on for quite sometime. This goes on to prove that street and working children have their own set of problems and need special care while dealing with them. They are sexually exploited and are also habituated of other evils like smoking, drugs and other addiction, which have very harmful effects. Thus need extra care and attention.

The inmates of the Night Shelter are generally happy being part of SBT family, since they prefer this sheltered/protected life to the free but lonely and difficult life of the railway station. However, there is discontentment over some trivial issues. For instance, some boys have problems regarding the food being served. The boys' education is sponsored by an American NGO, which sends money, gifts and letters to the sponsored child. The children feel that SBT cheats them by giving them only the gifts etc. and not the dollars sent by their sponsors. This kind of misunderstanding invokes the need of total transparency between beneficiaries and the benefactors. But whatever their grievances might be, they fully realise that their future is secure at the Shelter and not in the streets and hence they rightly continue to stay put here.

10.2 GRP Contact Point and Schools on Railway Platforms

GRP Contact Point was earlier called 'Nukkad'. It is a contact point nearest to the railway station. It is situated at the terrace of GRP Station. The police have accommodated the street children so that they be able to get an opportunity to study and enjoy whatever is left of their childhood. The social workers survey the railway station and persuade street and working children to attend classes either at GRP centre or at the Platform Schools of SBT. Younger boys are sent to the Night Shelter since they are vulnerable to exploitation of all sorts not only by senior boys and criminal elements but also by the police and army *jawans,* at the station. Efforts are also made to send those to their homes who realise that they were wrong in leaving their homes. But some boys do not want to go back home since they have left because of adverse family atmosphere or due to poverty. Some boys keep contact with their family and whenever they go home they take with them money for their family members.

The activities of GRP Centre include teaching children the basic literacy and numerals, developing their potential through recreational activities like drawing, painting, plays and poems, indoor games, viz., ludo, snakes-ladder, carom etc. This is one effort towards giving back their childhood, which is lost due to their daily struggles for survival. The children are also taught good hygiene habits, but the circumstances in which they live day in and day out there is no benefit of such training for them. Children coming here are also served free lunch.

The timing of GRP centre is from 10 a.m. to 2 p.m. Although some children come regularly at the centre, there are some, who have to be persuaded to come to the centre everyday. The main attraction for children here is free lunch and the opportunity to play. But some boys are really serious to study and have progressed to the extent to be able to read sign-boards in English compared to the times when they did not know reading and writing. The weekly time-table followed at the Centre is as given below. However, it is not very strictly followed and some flexibility is allowed.

- Monday – Report of the Activities of the Week
- Tuesday – T.V. Show.

  Movies and Documentaries are shown to boys on this day. These may either be just for entertainment or may have patriotic and educational contents, e.g., the documentaries may raise awareness regarding Child's Rights, problem of AIDS, and so on.

- Wednesday – Medical Day.
  Dr. George Bittra visits the Centre to check up the children's Medical Reports and to attend to the children's medical requirements.
- Thursday – Outing/Picnics.
  Children are taken out to picnics or educational tours to zoological parks or places of historical interest.
- Friday – Sports Day.
  Since the New Delhi Railway Station is a congested place and there are no parks nearby, boys are taken to India Gate lawns or to the Jawaharlal Nehru Stadium.
- Saturday – Children's Day.
  On Saturdays, children are free from studies and they recite poems, songs and stories to the class, or play ludo and carom among themselves.

A typical day at GRP centre begins with enquiring the children whether they have had a bath or not. Those who haven't are asked by the teacher/social worker to go for bath at the public bathrooms maintained by the agency "Sulabh", at the railway station. The accessibility to the "Sulabh public bathrooms" is through a chit issued by the concerned social worker of GRP Centre to the child, which bears the name of the child and the signature of the social worker. Children are given soaps for bathing and washing clothes. Those who have long nails are given nail-cutters to chop them. Children, who have some cuts/bruises or mild headaches/stomach-aches, are provided medicines. This is important since these children work in rough circumstances and cuts/bruises are part of their daily lives.

Later, the children are taught with the help of charts. However, there are many disturbances, since GRP staff keep on coming and going to their offices situated near the place where children study. At the same time, some boys too do not pay attention to studies and play carom in the class even on repeated pleas by the teacher and thus disturb the other boys who wish to study.

The children working at the Station are illegal porters and sometimes the police round them up to be sent to the Remand Homes. Thereafter, the social workers request the police that SBT is taking care of these boys and hence they should not be sent away. However, sometimes children are taken away without the notice of the social worker.

Thus, GRP Centre caters to a floating population of children workers who come and go, sometimes at their own will and sometimes forced due to circumstances.

The same is the case with the SBT's other Platform Schools, viz., Sunrise at platform No. 12 and Dreams at platform No. 5, the timings of which are from 8 a.m. to 10 a.m. Children can attend any of these Platform Schools. It is not necessary that children of one particular Platform School would attend the same school. However, due to their rapport with one particular social worker/teacher, they might like to come at the same school everyday.

All such children, i.e., those at the Night Shelter, GRP Centre or Platform Schools are either porters, vendors, rag-pickers or are shoe-shine boys. They have left their homes due to poverty, drunkard fathers, ill-treatment by step-mother/fathers or other guardians, or losing one's parents or on failing in the school. Some run away on not finding schools interesting since teachers beat them up or do not teach or make them do their personal works. Some children do keep contact with their families and pay a visit to their homes once they start earning at the Station. Some children who go away do not necessarily come back to Delhi, they might go to other cities or towns. Even in Delhi it likely that they may not come back to avail the benefits provided by SBT and they may go elsewhere. So, SBT tries to help children who are then and there so that the children may learn something till the limited time they are with SBT. However, since SBT is working at the railway station, it has not been able to provide the atmosphere that is required for studies. At the Platform Schools, there is too much of a noise due to the trains so much so that children and teacher are not able to make each others heard. Disturbance caused by GRP staff at GRP Centre has already been mentioned. Due to all this children are not able to concentrate. Even the social workers there complain of the bad working conditions. All this affects the good efforts being attempted by the SBT. This, however, do not deter children from attending the various Centres because it is here that they feel they belong and that there is somebody to take care of them.

10.3 The 24 Hour Drop-in-Shelter

Night Shelter caters to children below the age of 14 years and the older children of the railway station had no recourse to any Shelter. So in the year 1997, a 24 Hour Drop-in-Shelter was started where such children could drop in anytime, take rest, have a secure place to keep their belongings, undertake some kind of vocational training if they so wished and avail of the free medical services of SBT. It is situated near the railway station so as to maintain proximity to the children's place of work. Boys either come through GRP Centre, Platform Schools or from the Night Shelter (i.e., those boys who have become over-age in the Night Shelter are transferred to the Drop-in Shelter). The boys coming here are observed for one month and those who are found to be regular are registered in the Shelter and provided a locker to keep their belongings. The Shelter takes care of the educational needs of the boys making them at least capable to read and write. At the same time, medical needs of the boys are also taken care of. Those boys who are sick are provided free meals. The boys coming here are required to deposit Rs.5 of their earning at the Shelter, daily. The boys who wish to study further are helped by SBT in getting them admitted to the National Open School. SBT also helps them in acquiring training in different trades and crafts such as tailoring, automobile training, air-condition repair work, painting, typing and computer training. SBT has a linkage with 'Shramik Vidyapeeth[3]' where boys are sent for training. The vocational training is provided after consulting with the boys and depending on area of their interest. Such boys are also helped by SBT in job placements. Those, who wish to start small business, for instance, selling ice creams, are provided necessary help and investment. Since most of the boys availing the services of the Shelter are working, some even doing the night shifts, the timing of the NFE is from 2 p.m. to 4 p.m. Recreational activities are also encouraged here. Nothing is forced here since the boys are mature enough and know for them what is right. However, proper knowledge and guidance is given to them. Boys are also encouraged to save their money and those who open an account with the help of SBT are given an interest of Rs. 10/- on every Rs. 100/- saved. SBT also helps those boys who on getting a secure job wish to stay somewhere else. They are helped in finding a rented place and in getting some necessary household items.

10.4 Child Help Line Initiative

Knowing some history of the Child Line Service is imperative before we proceed to discuss SBT's efforts in this regard. Child Line was initiated in Mumbai in June 1996 by the Tata Institute of Social Sciences as an experimental project in collaboration with the Mahanagar Telephone Nigam Ltd., and 14 organisations working with children and was targeted specifically at street children. On October 1998 Child Line was launched at the national level. Impressed by the response received by street children in terms the number of calls for help that were received, the government decided to take the project under its wing and promised to sponsor its implementation.

Child Line is a phone outreach service committed to responding to children who need emergency assistance. This telephone service is free i.e., anyone can call at the telephone number 1098 to help a child in distress. For the proper functioning of this service Delhi has been divided into 5 zones North, South, East, West, Central, each handled by respectively Prayas, Butterflies, Delhi Brotherhood Society, Don Bosco and SBT. The areas coming under Central zones include: Paharganj, Connaught Place, ITO, Half of the Karol Bagh, Patel Nagar, Naraina Vihar, Tis Hazari, Red Fort, Subzi Mandi (Malka Ganj), Goldakhana, areas of Ram Manohar Lohia Hospital and India Gate. Since in the Central Delhi region, there are more of street children, whose primary requirement is of medical care, hence SBT deals with more cases regarding medical help.

SBT has employed two of its Night Shelter boys, who have completed their education, to manage the Child Line initially for the period of one year. These two boys are also being provided vocational training. After the expiry of their term, another set of SBT boys will be given the charge of Child Line. This arrangement not only helps to rehabilitate the boys but also in sympathetic handling of the calls of street children and in solving their problem since the SBT shelter boys have gone through the vagaries of street life and can understand the problems of other street and working children. Mostly the calls received from street and working children on Child Line are for medical help, for shelter, food, counselling, missing child and for repatriation/rehabilitation. There were nearly 400 medical calls. SBT has got admitted 15-16 distressed children in hospital who are undergoing long-term treatment there. It has rehabilitated 20 such children, whereas it has placed 15-20 street girls in different NGOs of Delhi, which takes care of the girl children. The Coordinator of Child Line informed about an interesting incident. SBT Child Line received a call from Chandni Chowk, (Balli Maran, Kaptan wali gali), informing that 2-3 children have been kept like slaves in the nickel factory there. The children were engaged in polishing nickel over iron. SBT team went there and sought the help of police at the Police Station there. But the police did not take any action till four hours. In the mean time the children were hidden away, so that on reaching the Nickel Factory, no child could be found. This goes on to prove the existence of a nexus between Police and the factory owners. SBT submitted its report to the Labour Ministry and also questioned the inaction of police.

11. Some Case Studies of Beneficiaries

11.1 Gulab Singh: Gulab Singh's is a story of a boy who would have died but for the timely medical help by the SBT. Gulab Singh has been a beneficiary of SBT since he was 11-years old. Right now he is 21 years old. He hails from Lucknow, has 2 brothers and 2 sisters and his father is a farmer. He ran away from his house when he failed in the exams in Class V and was afraid to face his father. He came to New Delhi Railway Station and started working as a coolie. There he met Barry John, one of the founders of SBT. Gulab Singh was persuaded to join Theatre and thus he started going to Mandi House for theatre education and used to get Rs. 15/- as stipend. This continued for 6 months. One day he was caught by the police and was taken to the Children's Home at Delhi Gate, there he stayed for 2 years but he ran away from there and again started to live at the Station. But now he got involved in bad company and started taking too much drugs so much so that both his lungs failed. He was brought to the SBT at the critical stage of lung failure. He was admitted to the Hospital where he underwent treatment. On getting discharged he joined SBT learning Centre. Working as a peon in a nearby office in Paharganj, till today he is undergoing treatment for his lung failure from the SBT Doctor.

11.2 Riyaz Ali: Riyaz Ali is 14 years old boy staying at the Night Shelter. He lost his parents when he was 7 years old and was being looked after by his brother and *Bhabhi* (sister-in-law) in Assam, when his mother's sister took him to Delhi in the Motia Khan slums. He was asked to work in a *Dhaba*, which involved backbreaking work from 5.30 in the morning till 5 O' clock in the evening, for a paltry sum of Rs. 300 per month. He worked there for 6 months. Then he came into contact with an NGO named Jagriti, which works, for the education of slum children of Motia Khan. There he studied till Class III. Riyaz Ali came to know about SBT from one of his friends at Jagriti and so he joined SBT since he wanted to stay away from his *Mausi*. Since then he is with SBT Night Shelter. Presently, he is in Class VII and aspires to be a motor mechanic. He likes the sheltered life at SBT. He also goes to meet his brother in Assam during school holidays.

11.3 Shamshad Alam: Shamshad Alam is a 12 years old boy from Bihar. At home he has left behind his father, mother and two elder sisters. He has learnt from his friend, hailing from the same village, that his parents have sold their land and moved away and now Alam desperately wants to know where his family is. He repents leaving his house but of no avail since he cannot go back to his family. When the authors interviewed him, he requested to write a letter to his grandmother asking her to inform him, at the SBT address, about the whereabouts of his parents.

His story goes like this. At the age of 6, he was admitted to the '*madarsa*' (Muslim learning centre), but he had hardly finished six months there that his father took him out of it since the teacher used to beat the children. Later he started learning the trade of repairing decks (music system) from his mother's brother. He also used to pick rags. On being persuaded by one of his friends, he ran away from home to Delhi by train. On reaching Delhi, for the initial 2-3 days he was totally lost as to what to do. On feeling hungry he used to ask for the leftovers from the attendants of the Rajdhani Express. He was also watching how other boys are surviving. One fine day, on being extremely hungry, he took out a big iron piece from the railway track and went to the trader frequented by the other rag picker boys. He sold the iron bar to the trader and earned Rs. 60. Since then, he is working as rag picker and earns by selling bottles. He came into contact with SBT through one of his friends at the station and now regularly attends GRP Centre. Though he likes reading and writing and to paint, he has a deep yearning to be with his family.

11.4 Sunny: Sunny is a 9-year-old bright young boy. He is in Delhi since 10-12 days. He left his home in Badarpur as his father used to beat him up. He took a bus to the New Delhi Railway Station and came here. Though his life is very difficult, sleeping at the Station, eating the leftovers, he is not interested to go back home. He is very eager to study and learns vcry fast. He was found studying at not only GRP Centre but also at the Platform School, which shows how eager he is to learn.

11.5 Santosh: Santosh is a 23-year lad hailing from Deoghar, Bihar. He is the youngest among his 4 brothers. He ran away at the age of 12, since his guardian (father's brother), used to beat him. From his village he went to Calcutta, there on to Ludhiana and then to Delhi. He has been lucky to get jobs wherever he went and faced no problems anywhere. At Delhi, he came into contact with Barry John of SBT who took him to Mandi House and taught him theatre art. There he did many plays. He boasts of knowing Manoj Bajpai, a T.V. and Cinema artist, very closely. On completing his education at the Night Shelter, he did many jobs. Nowadays, he is handling the Child Line and also getting trained in motor driving. He aspires to go to Bollywood but first he wants to save a lot of money so that he may be able to survive during his days of struggle in Mumbai.

11.6 Pappu: Pappu came to Delhi from Calcutta when he was 13 years old. At home he has his parents, 4 brothers and 3 sisters, he is the eldest. His father is a Railway Guard. He went to school till he was 8 years old, but lost interest in studies when his younger brother, whom he loved very much, died. He has tried his luck in a number of activities, including theatre, and often shuttles between Delhi and Mumbai. Right now, he is in the Drop-in-Shelter and is undergoing training in motor mechanics earning a stipend of Rs. 400/- per month.

12. Future Plans

The future plan of SBT[4] is as follows:

1. To initiate a programme for the working children in the Paharganj market area.
2. To enable the children working in *dhabas* and other interested

working children to establish and run a restaurant of their own.

3. To establish a Boarding School for rehabilitation and education of the runaway working children.
4. To initiate a project for the girl street child on the same lines as the boys project.
5. To increase the scope and coverage of the programmes and to strengthen the existing programmes.
6. To improve the availability of the medical facilities to the street and working children.

To this list, the Trustee, Ms. Nair, added two more plans:

1. SBT plans to start Door-step Schools. The concept of Door-step School is to reach out to the slum children at their slums with a special bus with no seats, with a black board and 2 volunteers. This bus will go from one slum to the other and teach the children so that they get accustomed to the idea of school and later they might be admitted to regular schools.
2. SBT also plans to initiate a project on entrepreneurship development for boys in the age group of 16-21 years in the slums where it is currently working. Along with it, it will also teach them facts on their sexuality like when to marry, how to space their children and other health aspects.

13. Achievements

In the course of more than a decade of its existence, SBT has been able to bring in 200-300 boys into the mainstream of life as drivers, computer programmers, tailors, export house workers, as courier boys and in theatres.

One of the SBT's boys, Harish, who has been with SBT since 1989, has been teaching theatre education in National School of Drama and is on Sanjoy's staff, showed a lot of interest in the Theatre. SBT has got him roles in T.V. Serials, in Films such as "Patanga" and "Bandit Queen". He has been trained through theatre workshops in the National School of Drama, Delhi.

According to the founder: "At least 50 human lives have been saved in all these years from Drugs, AIDS, anti-social activities. If we had not made the intervention, they could have become hardcore criminals. All boys of Shelter Home are going to the school. We want to start more shelters as soon as the local government gives space for accommodation".

14. Limitations

The Trustee of SBT, Mr. Sanjoy Roy, summarised the limitations or the difficulties in the progress of SBT's work as:

1. One of the major limitations for SBT is the societal apathy for the street and working children. Street and working children are most affected from the environment, in which they work and live. They suffer from character-disorder, it is a disability, which cannot be seen visually, and hence there is not much sympathy for them, as is the case with, for instance, the disabled children. Out of the 27 priority areas of work in the field of children, street children ranks at 23rd position (a very low priority). The work for helping these children requires sensitivity from the police, employers, government, social workers and the general public, which is rarely achieved. All runaway's children have the basic requirement of secure spaces and a secure childhood. Neither the NGOs perceive these needs and work in this area, nor do they have the required infrastructure to cope with the needs of street and working children. For instance, one very important need of children is proper places to play but there are not many spaces for that.
2. Another important problem faced by the organisation is of the shortage of efficient staff. It is generally the case that grassroots level social workers who are responsible for improving the lives of so many children, are worst paid. Due to this reason, such activities are not attracting the best people. Those who do not find any other work in the job-market generally take up such works.
3. There is also a lack of professional volunteer, i.e., people who are experts in the field of arts and crafts and who can

voluntarily teach the children and thus help them in finding a meaning for the childhood.

SBT has not been able to strike at the root of the problem of child labour nor is there any attempt towards it. As opposed to BMM, which is working towards banning child labourers of every category and want to usher in an equal social structure, SBT is focussed on one particular segment of child labour — the street and working children and is providing them help within the existing social structure. This has to do with the ideology adopted by the head of the organisation. In the next chapter, which presents the summary and conclusions, it has been illustrated, by taking the instances of SBT and BMM, as to how the ideology of the organisation affects the strategy it adopts to deal with the issue. It has also been shown in the forthcoming chapter how the very ideology limits the organisational ability to deal with the problem.

REFERENCES

1. Source: Brochure, SBT.
2. Source: Brochure, SBT.
3. The Government run vocational training institute,
4. Source: Brochure, SBT.

7

Restoring Child Rights
Summary and Recommendations

The analysis of NGOs activities for child labourers in Delhi shows that NGOs instead of acting as social change agents are acting as "service organisations", their main activity being provision of services. In the context of child labour, what is more important than the provision of services, is reformative programmes. Child labour is a social stigma. The government has not been able to abolish the system of child labour in India. The attitude that child labour is a necessary evil has resulted in perpetuating the problem. Voluntary effort by non-governmental organisations can help in advocacy of the cause by bringing pressure upon the system to correct itself. They have to call for a total elimination of the child labour system. Any strategy to deal with child labour will be successful if it puts the elimination of child labour on a non-negotiable agenda. Yet the main thrust of the non-governmental approach now is to provide relief at various levels to children who must work, in the form of non-formal schooling, technical education, recreational facilities, counselling, credit facilities, health care and issuing of identity cards for their protection.

The idea behind such protective strategies is that child labour cannot be legislated out of existence overnight. Although abolition remains the long-term goal, yet children need protection here and now and so the emphasis is on a broad range of practical measures in a number of areas. These include: education and training, advocacy and emphasis to promote public awareness, protective work schemes and regulation of work conditions.

The Ministry of Welfare, Government of India and UNICEF in its report of the First Asian Conference on Child Exploitation and Abuse,[1] presented the following typology of child labour projects.

Typology of Child Labour Projects

Type of Intervention	Child	Family	Community
Education and Training	• Access to schooling • Non-formal Education • Vocational Training	• Stipends • Adapting school hours to family needs • Convincing parents on value of education	• Provision of schooling and vocational training in community centres
Welfare Services	• Health monitoring • Supplementary nutrition • Access to health • Removal from hazardous work	• Health education • Social Security • Welfare support care • Income generation	• Provision of community health centres • Drop-in-centres
Protection Work	• Provision of safe environment tailored to the development needs of children • Work placement schemes and Sheltered workshops	• Information on improved working conditions • Pressure on employers • Legal information	• Provision of protected work schemes • Volunteer support
Advocacy/Public Awareness Campaigns	• Establishing contact using peers • Developing awareness of situation and rights • Developing self-representation • Use of mass media e.g., newspapers, magazines, radio, TV, puppet, theatre, comics	• Information on health and education • Legal information	• Citizen's groups • Community theatre • Mass media e.g. radio • Mobilise teachers, religious groups, voluntary organisation, employers' groups and trade-unions

Type of Intervention	**Child**	**Family**	**Community**
Regulation and Enforcement	• Raising awareness of labour laws • Report violations	• Educating families concerning the law and their responsibilities • Birth registration	• Mobilising trade unions on behalf of unorganised and marginal workers • Educating employers on the law and work effects on children • Citizen's committees and pressure groups for enforcement

Our study of the protection and rehabilitation of child labourers by NGOs also more or less, conforms to the above typology. These initiatives being undertaken by the 17 NGOs studied may be summarised under the two heads, viz., protective and regulative work and release/rescue and mass sensitisation work. We have given the term "protectionist" NGOs, which are involved in the former types of activities, while those involved in the latter type of activities have been called "radical" NGOs.

Briefly, the initiatives being taken by the NGOs that were surveyed and as discussed in chapter 4, under the above heads are as follows:

Protective and Regulative Work

1. Provision of non-formal education (NFE) with free uniforms, books, library facility and incentives of mid-day meals. Social issues are often woven in the curriculum. After the completion of their NFEs, the children are helped in getting an affidavit or the Birth Certificate (required for getting admission into the regular school) and put into Municipal Corporation of Delhi (MCD) Schools.
2. Along with the NFE, children are also imparted vocational training, in such crafts/trades as carpentry, book binding, sweet boxes making, candle making, scooter repairing, in-house wiring, cutting and tailoring, embroidery and beauty culture. Children are allowed to choose the vocations, which suits their own interests.
3. The NGOs also concentrate their effort on upgrading the self-confidence and self-esteem of these children as the latter have a very low esteem. Children are encouraged to speak for themselves and about their problems.
4. Shelter Homes with lodging and boarding, schooling, vocational training and recreational facilities, are provided for the runaway children. Night Shelters, 24-hours Drop-in Centres, Crèche and Outreach Centres are provided to cater to the needs of a safe and secure place for these children.
5. Savings-scheme for child workers, initiating credit unions and cooperatives to mobilise and empower child workers. Attempt is also made to regulate the working conditions by

providing the rag picker children with sunglasses, gloves, by forming for them a cooperative so that they can work in a systematic and hygienic way.

6. Giving street children Identity Cards so that they feel secure and have a sense of belonging to the organisation concerned.
7. Providing counselling services to children and their parents.
8. Providing legal help to street and working children in case of emergencies.
9. Community development programmes, which includes such components as education, health, income-generation and community organisation.
10. Programmes on personal health, hygiene and sexuality. The Doctors and Health Specialists of the NGOs conduct regular health check-ups for these children. For the serious cases, the NGOs have linkages with the government hospitals, where such cases are looked after.
11. Conducting research studies on child labour — its magnitude, causes and consequences, to have a better understanding of the problem so as to devise good policy alternatives.
12. Sponsorship programmes for helping the disadvantaged children who need a sponsor, a special parent, who could help them through the organisation to meet their basic needs like education, books, tuition, health care and nutrition. Some organisations market their cards and profit from it is utilised for the needy children.

Release, Rescue and Mass Sensitisation Work

1. Conducting raids and rescue operations to release child labourers from the so-called hazardous industries, such as fireworks, glass factories, carpet weaving, mining, diamond cutting and polishing and the like.
2. Mass sensitisation through holding Seminars, Conferences, rallies, marches, wall writing and demonstrations. Telecasting TV commercials on what they themselves are doing for child labourers and to raise awareness on child labour.
3. Conducting consumer campaign to mobilise the consumers not to use the products such as fire-works, carpets etc., made

by children. Launching a 'Global Campaign' to highlight the need to rise against the practice of child labour. It is the result of these efforts that World Bank has made a decision to stop the aid if they find child labour in any of the projects they are funding.

4. Advocacy with political parties to persuade them to include the issue of elimination of child labour, promise of free and compulsory education, in their election manifestos. Also lobbying at the policy level by organising regional, national and international level seminars, workshops and conferences.

"Radical" NGOs believe that it is not sufficient to just providing relief to the child labourers. One has to strike at the very root cause of the problem of child labour. In order to achieve this, besides releasing, rescuing and rehabilitating child labourers, these NGOs get engrossed in reforming the existing unequal structure of the society by fighting against the social problems like the caste system, the bonded labour system and alcoholism, that causes and perpetuates child labour.

Reform is needed when a part of the community (child labourers in this case), continues to be socially and/or economically exploited by others. Often such exploitation is also supported by the traditional social structure and the continuous deprivation of the exploited group. Therefore, one could expect enormous resistance on the part of those who exploit the children to meet their selfish ends. In this regard, one could also conduct research to assess the efficacy of various welfare programmes/schemes implemented by the government and utilise the finding to initiate reforms in such programmes. It is obvious, however, that such attempt to reform the social structure or an apathetic administration is always resented by those on the top of the system.

The irony of the situation is that, aided with the popular support, NGOs are in the best position to attempt such programmes. Yet such interventions are lacking, as is evident from the study that out of 17 NGOs studied only two of them, viz. BMM and SACCS, are challenging the basic system of inequality prevalent in the Indian society.

The "protectionist" organisations believe that the working children need support to meet their educational, nutritional, health and vocational needs. They also believe that these children need skills and information necessary to earn a living wage and fight for their rights to survive with dignity. These organisations, just like the "radical" organisations, consider child labour as bad and exploitative. However, their strategy of dealing with the problem differs significantly. They, instead of joining together to create a revolution in the society against child labour, want to wait for the situation when child labour is totally eliminated and until then, they prefer to fulfill the working children's needs of "food, security, health, love and education, a place to play and perchance to dream".

The study reveals that it is the ideology adopted by an organisation, which defines the particular approach/strategy adopted towards the problem. The advocates of the radical ideology recommend abolishing all forms of child labour immediately. They argue that in the long run, developing countries, like India, would benefit both economically and socially from a public policy of strict enforcement of compulsory education and minimum age laws. They maintain that India has the resources for greater investment in education but lack the necessary political will. They believe that strict enforcement of both compulsory education and child labour laws would be much easier to administer than a more differentiated system and would reduce opportunities for corruption.

Those with the protectionist ideology — majority of them as is evident from the study — believe that the immediate abolition of child labour is unrealistic and, in many cases, contrary to the interests of the children themselves. They recommend that instead of an outright ban on child labour, initially only the most abusive forms of child labour should be abolished, while the remaining forms of child labour should be strictly regulated, to provide appropriate protection and benefits for those who must work to survive.

These two ideologies and strategies are represented by BMM and SBT, the case studies of which we have attempted. BMM represents the former ideology of eradication of child labour while SBT represents the latter ideology of protection and rehabilitation of child labour. BMM is founded by an Arya Samaji protagonist, Swami Agnivesh, who strives for an equal, just and exploitation free society. Child labour is seen here as part of the larger system of inequality and exploitation — exploitation of lower classes by the upper classes (class inequality) and exploitation of lower castes by the upper castes (caste inequality).

So the organisation views child labour in a wider socio-economic milieu.

On the other hand SBT views child labour as an economic problem. It believes that child labour exists due to poverty of parents, which forces them to engage their children in work to supplement family income. SBT was founded by Praveen Nair belonging to an economically well off family, who had philanthropic inclination of helping the poor and needy children. Hence, her organisation is more of a "service organisation".

Since their approach to view the problem is totally different the strategies of SBT and BMM also differ. BMM is engaged in conducting raids, rescue and rehabilitation of bonded child labourers as also attempting to reform the social structure by fighting social evils such as the caste and gender inequality, religious bigotry and alcoholism. For children who have been free from the bondage of child labour, BMM opens up informal schools with the incentive of a packet of biscuit for each schooling day. This is aimed to develop in these children the habit of going to the school. BMM has opened up 8 such schools in Faridabad. The children studying here belong to parents whom BMM had released from the bondage of stone quarry owners around two decades ago. BMM has formed a union of stone quarry workers which has helped them raise their voice against exploitation by quarry owners. It has also made arrangements to settle down the workers near the quarries/mines with the provision of ration, drinking water and health facilities. By opening up schools, BMM tries to demonstrate the fact that poor people, in spite of their poverty, want to and do send their children to school, thus, exploding the myth that child labour exists since poor parents want their children to work and earn for the family.

On the other hand, SBT was started to take care of children who have run away from home due to either poverty, ill treatment of step-parents, alcoholic fathers or any other reason and who land up on the streets where they have to work for their survival. The objective of the organisation is to bring a difference in the lives of street and working and try and bring them into the mainstream. It also to tries to give them back the childhood, which they have lost as they have to earn their living at a tender age. Hence, SBT's activities revolve around providing the basic needs of a shelter, nutrition, medical help, counselling, recreation, non-formal and primary education to the street and working children. As such, SBT has established drop-in-shelters for those children who work at the railway platforms to provide homeless child with warmth at night, toilet and bath facilities, recreation and counselling services. For those homeless children who want to leave their work and have a brighter future, SBT has shelter homes to provide for their boarding-lodging, educational and recreational requirements. Such a strategy for street and working children is basically ameliorative in nature and do not aim to prevent the occurrence of the problem.

Just as the ideology of an organization shapes the strategy or approach adopted towards the problem, ideology also acts as a limiting factor on the practical operation of the strategy adopted. This is evident from the study of BMM and SBT. BMM is more ideological than practical. It combines a movement with an organisation. It embraces within its ambit besides child labour, a number of social issues like casteism, gender inequality, religious fundamentalism, corruption, alcoholism, increasing influence of westernised life-styles. Actually, BMM is more of a movement because it pays less attention to the organisational matters and more on the mobilization dimension. While it seems to be successful in generating awareness, it however does not seem to have paid attention to the nuts and bolt aspects. Although, the idea behind taking up so many activities is to reform the unequal structure of society, it becomes practically difficult to operate on such a wide scale with shortage of financial resources and efficient and dedicated manpower.

Swami Agnivesh, the charismatic social reformer, who runs the organisation, feels that like him the other members of society will accomplish the tasks of social reform by will, dedication and a drive for it. But in reality, there are very few volunteers, those who do, come and go according to their whims. There is an increasing need for professional and trained personnel to undertake the above activities, which in turn needs financial resources. However, there are few donors, who are interested in giving money for social reform since it does not have a demonstration effect, the impact cannot be quantified. Donors want to have figures of how many child labourers have been released, rescued and rehabilitated. They are not interested whether the community as a whole has become sensitised or not about the perils of the problem of child labour. Also this latter kind of work leads to challenging of the status quo. The awareness-building exercise and the mobilisation of the masses necessarily lead to a conflict with the state, preventing the donors from keeping away from such activities.

Thus, due to the shortage of funds, BMM has to make do with personnel who do not have technical and professional education and training and hence the quality of work suffers. Whatever little impact the organisation has been able to make is because of the charisma of its leader.

On the other hand, SBT, in contrast to BMM, has employed professional and trained social workers, psychologists, doctors, and nurses. However, the founder of SBT, Praveen Nair's idea to help the runaway children by working with them in their own milieu, is not able to have the desired effect of returning to the children their lost childhood. (This is not to deny the fact that SBT has been able to leave a mark on the lives of the children with whom it is working, as is evident from the case histories of the children provided in Chapter 6). One of the basic reasons for it is that the staff has practical problems in dealing with such street and working children who become mature at early age. The staff not only have to brave the harsh environment of the railway station, where these children work, but also have to be deal with the distorted perceptions and psyche of these children. They have to physically touch the children who may be suffering from infectious disease and in turn acquire the disease. All these practical considerations make them look for better opportunities elsewhere. The commitment to the cause and the dedication that the founder has for the children could not be found in majority of the staff. As a result the organisational goals cannot be fully realised.

The failure to realise the goals by both these organisations studied is also linked to the fact that the basic aims of the organisation have not been absorbed by the workers/staff who look upon themselves as professionals or persons doing a paid job. Part of the blame lies with the organisational heads who are not able to communicate their ideology to each and every member of the staff. The organisation thus represents not teamwork but one-personality structures with every possibility of dying out with the charisma of the founder.

The NGO's study also reveals that just as lack of committed and dedicated workers limits NGOs activities in the same way the apathetic attitude of the government towards the problem also acts as a limiting factor. Lack of political and administrative will, due to the nexus between employers, politicians and bureaucrat, leads to non-implementation of laws against child labour. This impairs the activities of BMM (representative of radical NGOs) engaged in the release and rescue of child labourers. On the other hand SBT faces the problem of unsympathetic attitude of police officials who harass children whom the organisation is trying to help. This calls for increasing cooperation and support of the government and the administrative system of NGOs who are trying to fulfill the task that the government should have been doing.

What More can be Done: Suggestions and Recommendations

At this juncture, we are in a position to put forth certain suggestions as to what more can be done in the area of combating child labour by NGOs and how government can facilitate the working NGOs. The suggestions also include the opinions of the personnel of the NGOs studied.

What the Government should Do?

1. The Government should make it clear whether it wants to eliminate child labour or just protect and regulate it. Also it should bring about a clarity in the definition of child labour since many of the organisations are not clear on who constitutes child labour and children upto what age can be called child labour.
2. A total ban should be imposed on every category of child labour and there should be a stricter punishment for those who employ children. For this more of *Bal Adalats* (Children's Courts) and Summary Trials with snap decisions should be held.
3. A comprehensive Child Labour Act should be devised and implemented.
4. The existing laws e.g., the Child Labour Protection (and Regulation) Act, 1986 and the Minimum Wages Act should be revised. The 1986 Act makes a distinction between hazardous and non-hazardous industries and talks of banning

child labour in the hazardous industries with the exclusion of child labour in the non-hazardous industries. However, for children, any kind of work, which hampers their physical, mental and social development, is hazardous.

5. The Minimum Wages Act, 1978 is very old and needs revision. This is important because if the head of the family were earning well, their children would not have to work. Also there should be uniformity in Minimum Wages in the different parts of the country. (For instance in Delhi, the Minimum Wage is Rs. 75, in Haryana it is Rs. 56, in Rajasthan it is Rs. 35 while in Orissa, the Minimum Wage is Rs. 25). For this a 'National Minimum Wage' (as demanded by Bandhua Mukti Morcha), should be introduced in the country, which should be equivalent to the first day salary of the IV Grade Government employees and be applied uniformly in all the States and the Union Territories. It should also be revised according to the cost-price index, as it is done for the Government employees.
6. The State Governments should fix up the wages for the unorganised labour and it should not be below the 'National Minimum Wages'.
7. The Government should improve and upgrade the standards of its educational institutions and make education more meaningful to decrease the dropout rate in schools managed by it.
8. It should also allocate a lot of resources for the education of the children.[2] This is necessary because education is the tool to wean children away from the work force.
9. The staff of the government schools should be sensitised to be sympathetic towards the street and working children, so that they do not harass the NGOs unnecessarily when the latter brings such children for admission in these schools.
10. Government should respect the views of those NGOs, which are dedicated to the cause of child labour and have done exemplary work in this field and should involve them at the policy planning level.
11. The Government should tap print and electronic media to educate people on the gravity of the problem of the child

labour and should make it loud and clear that employing the children is an offence. The coverage by media of child labour will increase awareness and consciousness amongst policy makers and others.

What More is Required of NGOs

1. More and more work by the NGOs should be at the grassroots level.
2. NGOs should concentrate more on the proper rehabilitation of the released child labourers.
3. Their focus of the work should be on children working in hazardous industries and occupations, bonded child labourers, street children, and those in the informal sectors, especially the *dhaba* and domestic workers.
4. The initiatives of NGOs should focus on the families of the child labourers as well. Among other things, the NGOs' efforts should be directed towards the use of adults productively since it is because of adult unemployment that children have to work.
5. The cooperation of the employers should be sought and they should be asked to spare the children, working with them, for at least 4 hours for their education and skill development.
6. Education should be imparted on a much larger scale. Instead of providing an alternative system of education and creating new schools for the working children, NGOs should pressurise the government to improve and raise the standard of education of the existing government schools.
7. The NGOs should take care of the nutritional needs of the poor children since they are undernourished. The NGOs should realise that the food requirement of the needy children can be fulfilled at very minimal cost.[3] Therefore, providing at least one full meal to the children per day should be part of their programme for children.
8. The vocational training imparted to the child labourers or potential child labourers should be compatible (in terms of remuneration), to the existing income-generating activities already being done by these children. For instance, if a child

is earning Rs.70 from rag picking he/she would not like to learn a craft or trade, which would fetch lesser money, than he/she is already earning.

9. The NGOs should provide for in their budget proposal the cost of monitoring of the projects. This is important since inadequate monitoring and follow-ups of the programmes and projects undertaken, leads to creating only a temporary effect.
10. Apart from focussing attention on the release and rehabilitation of children working in those industries with concentration of child labour, there is also the need to strike at the root of the problem by trying to improve the conditions of the "catchment areas", i.e., those areas from which these children migrate. This can be done through converging and targeting the different rural development programmes of the government in these areas.[4] For the urban areas, the NGOs should utilise the Urban Development Programmes of the government for the poor urban children.
11. NGOs should learn from the successful educational and other strategies like that of the M.V. Foundation. They should also learn from the child labour studies conducted by researchers. For instance, most studies on child labour in different industries[5] (matches and fireworks, lock, the carpet, etc.) have emphasized the need for a strategy, which addresses the survival questions of the family along with a package of education and health.

These gaps in action by the government and the NGOs also reflect their limitations, which among other things, flow out of the fact that especially in the care of children, one can supplement efforts made by families but cannot supplant it. The government as well as the NGOs in their enthusiasm for the advocacy for the child's rights of survival, development (provision), protection and participation, as enshrined in the UN Convention of Child Rights (1989), undermines the role of the parents and family in shaping the views of the child and thereby in the child's socialization. Here we may take the case of SBT. The organization by choosing street children, concentrates on the rehabilitation of working children and does not seek to change the existing unequal structure that produces street children. Even then it faces formidable obstacles — some internal to NGOs and some external. This goes on to prove the relevance of family as an institution and the way it takes care of the children. Thus, the family, as a fundamental group of society and the natural environment for the growth and well being of all its members and particularly children, should be afforded the necessary protection and assistance so that it can fully assume its responsibilities within the community.

The policy initiatives, therefore, should focus on the families of child labourers as well. Thus, a multi-pronged approach, the core of which would be to address the poverty of the families along with a package of health and education is called for.

Also, the government should take the ultimate responsibility of abolishing the system of child labour since it has the resources, administration and planning machinery. The working of NGOs is constrained by a number of factors, some internal and some external. For instance, NGOs have the problem of high turn over because of uncertainty that surrounds them. They do not have enough funds to recruit permanent employees, to give all the benefits/perks like provident fund, gratuity, and the like, as in the government sector.

Although, the introduction of professionals has become very important for NGOs for the efficacy of their programmes and projects, it requires on the part of NGOs a larger investment in administrative and infrastructure, which is not obtained. Because of the scarcity of funds, NGOs cannot retain professionals for long.

Still, NGOs have played a vital role in terms of advocacy of issues, like that of child labour, women's empowerment, tribal groups, construction of big dams at the cost of dislocating people, and the like. The case of BMM may also be cited here. BMM has advocated for compulsory primary education and has been able to raise awareness for education among the ex-bonded labourers, who set up a school on their own as discussed in Chapter 5. This is a remarkable achievement.

However, in the long run, only certain leaders of some NGOs can set up good examples, because of the charisma of the leader. But such charismatic personalities cannot be everywhere. There are only a few dedicated and committed people with ideologies. And the NGO dies down with the fading of charisma of such people.

In the final analysis, what we can say is that NGOs with their limited resources, can only provide models for replication at a large scale by the government. They cannot replace the government. They can give suggestions to the government while the latter should the implementing agency. NGOs can help in finding gaps in public action. They can also help the government in fulfilling its tasks. This is possible if the government develops faith in NGOs and channelises funds for the said purpose through the NGOs. They in turn, can mobilise, better expertise than the government and probably thus accomplish the tasks entrusted to them more efficiently. Obviously, the private sector has several advantages over the public sector. Flexibility in decision-making, quick execution, employment of trained hands, instead of routine bureaucrats is some of these.

But NGOs work on a double-edged sword. The government may use NGOs to supplement its efforts when its organs are not able to deliver the goods, or when sensitive data have to be collected. However, if NGOs become more successful than the government, the latter becomes apprehensive and may try to suppress NGO activity. Sometimes, even NGOs, in course of their functioning, may get too close to the government and may even absorb its identity to it, which totally goes against the goals for which the NGOs might be in existence. NGOs, thus, have to constantly try to retain its autonomy at the same time cooperating with the government.

The raison d'etre of voluntary organisations lies in the failure of the system to address itself to all the needs of a society as influenced and defined by the social consciousness obtained at a point of time in that society. And this gives the former its rationale, too: to perform functions, which the "system" fails to perform.

However, the NGO scenario at present is not that promising. What we see today is that the NGOs emphasise projects, not movements. They "mobilise" people to produce at the margins but not to struggle to control the basic means of production and wealth. They focus on technical and financial assistance for projects, not on structural conditions that shape the everyday lives of the people. The NGOs adopt the language of the left like "popular power", "empowerment", "gender equality" and "sustainable development". The problem is that this language is linked to framework of collaboration with donors and government agencies that subordinate practical activities to non-confrontational politics. The NGOs compete with the socio-political movements for influence among the poor, women and the racially excluded. Their ideologies and practices divert attention from the sources of poverty and its radical solutions.

Despite these limitations, NGOs have an important role to play in the protection and eradication of child labour. But, they will have to adopt a different approach if they really want eradication of child labour. Firstly, they will have to interact with each other to put up a collective demand on the basis of their common approach. Secondly, they will have to lobby to pressurise the government to accept the time-bound goal of banning child labour from all activities and to ratify the ILO Convention No. 138 for the purpose, which establishes that no child can be employed in any economic sector below the age designated for the completion of compulsory education and not less than 15 years. Thirdly, they will have to be vigilant about the enforcement of government regulations regarding child labour. And fourthly, they will have to join hands with other outside organisations to create a pressure group at the international level. They will have to shake away their apathy and take up the challenge 'boldly'. NGOs should attempt to create a movement against the exploitation of the poor, which will ultimately lead to pro-poor decision-making and pro-poor implementation of these decisions. In other words, NGOs can contribute significantly towards the creation of the much-wanted political will in the developing countries.

At the same time, a wide scope exists for complementary efforts by government and non-governmental organisations. Each has strengths and weaknesses and the trick is to arrive at a formula – which can reinforce and build on their respective strengths. NGOs can, for example, be effective in advocacy, organising communities and implementing small local projects. The government can focus on establishment of conducive legislative and policy climate, the provision of universal compulsory education, increasing the access of poor households to employment and income, and ensuring strict adherence to certain minimum labour standards such as the prohibition of work in hazardous occupations or activities, and work before the completion of primary schools. The respective functions and roles of government and non-government organisations cannot be viewed statically, these should develop and evolve within the framework of a partnership if they are to have, as indeed they must, a sustained impact on the condition of working children.

REFERENCES

1. "Child Exploitation and Abuse: A Global Phenomenon", The Report of the First Asian Conference on Child Exploitation and Abuse, Calcutta, 17-19 December 1990, Sponsored by Ministry of Welfare, Government of India and UNICEF.
2. As suggested by the Director, Deepalaya.
3. According to the General Secretary of Street Survivors India, the food requirement of the needy children can be met with such a minimal cost of Rs. 3.50 per child.
4. As told by the Director, Butterflies.
5. Vasanthi Raman, "Politics of Childhood: Perspectives from the South", Economic and Political Weekly, November 11, 2000, p 4058.

Index